OPPOSING
VIEWPOINTS®
SERIES

Gender in the
21st Century

Other Books of Related Interest

Opposing Viewpoints Series

Feminism
Identity Politics
The #MeToo Movement
Toxic Masculinity

At Issue Series

Campus Sexual Violence
Gender Politics
Male Privilege
Reproductive Rights

Current Controversies Series

Are There Two Americas?
Historical Revisionism
LGBTQ Rights
Microaggressions, Safe Spaces, and Trigger Warnings

"Congress shall make no law … abridging the freedom of speech, or of the press."

First Amendment to the US Constitution

The basic foundation of our democracy is the First Amendment guarantee of freedom of expression. The Opposing Viewpoints series is dedicated to the concept of this basic freedom and the idea that it is more important to practice it than to enshrine it.

OPPOSING
VIEWPOINTS®
SERIES

| Gender in the
| 21st Century

M. M. Eboch, Book Editor

GREENHAVEN
PUBLISHING

Published in 2020 by Greenhaven Publishing, LLC
353 3rd Avenue, Suite 255, New York, NY 10010

Cover image: Dn Br/Shutterstock.com

Library of Congress Cataloging-in-Publication Data

Names: Eboch, M. M., author.
Title: Gender in the 21st century / M.M. Eboch.
Description: New York : Greenhaven Publishing, [2019] | Series: Opposing
  viewpoints | Includes bibliographical references and index. | Audience:
  Grade 9 to 12.
Identifiers: LCCN 2019021541 | ISBN 9781534505933 (library binding) | ISBN
  9781534505926 (paperback)
Subjects: LCSH: Gender identity--Juvenile literature. | Sex differences
  (Psychology)--Juvenile literature. | Sex role--Juvenile literature.
Classification: LCC HQ1075 .E246 2019 | DDC 305.3--dc23
LC record available at https://lccn.loc.gov/2019021541

Manufactured in the United States of America

Website: http://greenhavenpublishing.com

Contents

Chapter 1: What Is Gender?

Chapter 2: What Is the Future of Femininity?

The Importance of Opposing Viewpoints

Perhaps every generation experiences a period in time in which the populace seems especially polarized, starkly divided on the important issues of the day and gravitating toward the far ends of the political spectrum and away from a consensus-facilitating middle ground. The world that today's students are growing up in and that they will soon enter into as active and engaged citizens is deeply fragmented in just this way. Issues relating to terrorism, immigration, women's rights, minority rights, race relations, health care, taxation, wealth and poverty, the environment, policing, military intervention, the proper role of government—in some ways, perennial issues that are freshly and uniquely urgent and vital with each new generation—are currently roiling the world.

If we are to foster a knowledgeable, responsible, active, and engaged citizenry among today's youth, we must provide them with the intellectual, interpretive, and critical-thinking tools and experience necessary to make sense of the world around them and of the all-important debates and arguments that inform it. After all, the outcome of these debates will in large measure determine the future course, prospects, and outcomes of the world and its peoples, particularly its youth. If they are to become successful members of society and productive and informed citizens, students need to learn how to evaluate the strengths and weaknesses of someone else's arguments, how to sift fact from opinion and fallacy, and how to test the relative merits and validity of their own opinions against the known facts and the best possible available information. The landmark series Opposing Viewpoints has been providing students with just such critical-thinking skills and exposure to the debates surrounding society's most urgent contemporary issues for many years, and it continues to serve this essential role with undiminished commitment, care, and rigor.

The key to the series's success in achieving its goal of sharpening students' critical-thinking and analytic skills resides in its title—

Opposing Viewpoints. In every intriguing, compelling, and engaging volume of this series, readers are presented with the widest possible spectrum of distinct viewpoints, expert opinions, and informed argumentation and commentary, supplied by some of today's leading academics, thinkers, analysts, politicians, policy makers, economists, activists, change agents, and advocates. Every opinion and argument anthologized here is presented objectively and accorded respect. There is no editorializing in any introductory text or in the arrangement and order of the pieces. No piece is included as a "straw man," an easy ideological target for cheap point-scoring. As wide and inclusive a range of viewpoints as possible is offered, with no privileging of one particular political ideology or cultural perspective over another. It is left to each individual reader to evaluate the relative merits of each argument— as he or she sees it, and with the use of ever-growing critical-thinking skills—and grapple with his or her own assumptions, beliefs, and perspectives to determine how convincing or successful any given argument is and how the reader's own stance on the issue may be modified or altered in response to it.

This process is facilitated and supported by volume, chapter, and selection introductions that provide readers with the essential context they need to begin engaging with the spotlighted issues, with the debates surrounding them, and with their own perhaps shifting or nascent opinions on them. In addition, guided reading and discussion questions encourage readers to determine the authors' point of view and purpose, interrogate and analyze the various arguments and their rhetoric and structure, evaluate the arguments' strengths and weaknesses, test their claims against available facts and evidence, judge the validity of the reasoning, and bring into clearer, sharper focus the reader's own beliefs and conclusions and how they may differ from or align with those in the collection or those of their classmates.

Research has shown that reading comprehension skills improve dramatically when students are provided with compelling, intriguing, and relevant "discussable" texts. The subject matter of these collections could not be more compelling, intriguing, or urgently relevant to today's students and the world they are poised to inherit. The anthologized articles and the reading and discussion questions that are included with them also provide the basis for stimulating, lively, and passionate classroom debates. Students who are compelled to anticipate objections to their own argument and identify the flaws in those of an opponent read more carefully, think more critically, and steep themselves in relevant context, facts, and information more thoroughly. In short, using discussable text of the kind provided by every single volume in the Opposing Viewpoints series encourages close reading, facilitates reading comprehension, fosters research, strengthens critical thinking, and greatly enlivens and energizes classroom discussion and participation. The entire learning process is deepened, extended, and strengthened.

For all of these reasons, Opposing Viewpoints continues to be exactly the right resource at exactly the right time—when we most need to provide readers with the critical-thinking tools and skills that will not only serve them well in school but also in their careers and their daily lives as decision-making family members, community members, and citizens. This series encourages respectful engagement with and analysis of opposing viewpoints and fosters a resulting increase in the strength and rigor of one's own opinions and stances. As such, it helps make readers "future ready," and that readiness will pay rich dividends for the readers themselves, for the citizenry, for our society, and for the world at large.

Introduction

> *"Much of the objection to change in gender roles is really about gender and power, not just about gender."*
>
> —Laura Liswood, *"Here's Why Gender Equality Is Taking So Long,"* World Economic Forum, September 20, 2017.

Throughout most of human history, societies around the world have divided people into two groups: men and women. Until the first half of the twentieth century, both science and philosophy assumed that gender corresponded to sex. Furthermore, most people accepted traditional gender roles for men and women. Men should have a masculine appearance and do masculine jobs. Women should have a feminine appearance and do feminine work. Most people believe these assigned roles were based on the physical and mental abilities of each sex.

Then French feminist Simone de Beauvoir published *The Second Sex* in 1949. She separated the biology of sex from the concept of gender. Sex comes from the physical characteristics of the body. Gender reflects society's opinions about what men and women should be. As such, gender can change over time and across cultures.

Beauvoir and the feminists who followed her argued that biology is not destiny. Women could overcome the perceived limitations of their sex. They could define their own identities. These feminists imagined a world where people were not defined by gender. They wanted a society that would not make assumptions based on a person's biology.

Later scholars and activists adapted these arguments to new views of gender. Gender freedom could lead to more rights for people who were intersex (born with features of both sexes) or transgender. It allowed people across the LGBTQ spectrum to embrace the word "queer." Previously, the term generally meant homosexual. Now it encompasses anyone whose gender and/or sexual orientation falls outside of the heterosexual norm. This revolution brought freedom to people who felt trapped in the wrong body or oppressed by society's gender standards.

The dismantling of gender brought confusion to others. Some people resist change for religious or political reasons. Others are simply uncomfortable with ideas that challenge what they previously learned. Resistance can also come from those who fear a loss of power. Embracing ideals of freedom and equality benefits oppressed people. Those ideals ask the people currently holding power to give up their privileges.

In addition, change can happen quickly for individuals but slowly for systems. Most government forms don't have options for people who don't want to declare a gender. It's easy to come up with new gender-neutral pronouns, such as zie. It's not so easy to get people used to using those new words.

Today, the gender wars have reached a new level. People fiercely debate whether marriage should be limited to a man and a woman. They argue over who should be allowed to use which bathrooms. They even clash over the very concept of gender. Does it depend on the biological sex at birth? Or is it mental and emotional, only sometimes matching biology? Can it change over time? Can somebody have no gender at all?

The world, at least the Western world, is seeing a trend toward dismantling old ideas of gender. In this new view, one's identity is not determined by biology, genes, or upbringing. Rather, identity comes from how people see themselves. How far will this go? Will most people choose to stay in traditional masculine and feminine roles? Will society eventually eliminate the very ideas of male and female? If so, will the future be the ideal dreamed of by some, or the collapse of society feared by others?

Scott Yenor, a professor of political science at Boise State University, addressed this in an essay for The Heritage Foundation. "Many Americans today have accepted what seemed inconceivable just a generation ago: that gender is artificial, is socially constructed, and can be chosen freely by all individuals.... Yesterday's shocking theory has become today's accepted norm, with more changes to come. Yet whether this new world will prove to be fit for human flourishing remains to be seen."

The questions surrounding what gender is, and what it can be or should be, give rise to vigorous debate. In chapters titled "What Is Gender?" "What Is the Future of Femininity?" "What Is the Future of Masculinity?" and "What Is the Future of Gender?" the authors of the viewpoints in *Opposing Viewpoints: Gender in the 21st Century* examine the current state of gender and offer perspectives from all sides of the issues.

CHAPTER 1

What Is Gender?

Chapter Preface

The way people perceive gender is changing. This leads to questions about how to define gender. What is the difference between a person's sex and their gender? What does it mean to be male or female? What does it mean to be masculine or feminine? Are people born to their gender, or is it an arbitrary social concept?

The question can be addressed from many angles. Biology studies the physical body and its processes. Neuroscience studies the brain and nervous system. In these fields, scientists can identify average differences between the sexes. However, they also see overlap in many areas. Males and females have typical differences but without a strict division.

Other researchers look at gender from the point of view of sociology. They study differences between cultures and across time periods. Those who study human society do not always agree on the causes and meaning of gender. Some feel that men and women should have different roles in society, because they have traditionally had different roles. Men fight, women protect. Who are modern people to try to change thousands of years of behavior? Yet others point out cultural and historical gender differences. They claim this proves that gender is merely a social construct: Society imposes masculine and feminine behavior on people. Dividing people into only two groups denies the vast variety of individual differences. Why should people be slaves to their genitals?

Do gender roles benefit or hinder people in modern society? Younger generations seem inclined to refuse traditional roles. Some people do not identify with either traditional gender. Others identify as male or female but refuse to behave in traditionally masculine or feminine ways. And yet, most young people are still being raised with traditional gender roles. They feel they should be masculine or feminine. They try to conform, even if those behaviors cause anxiety and unhappiness.

What is the future of gender? Will most people choose to be masculine or feminine while a few break out of traditional roles? Will society as a whole reject the idea of only two genders? Will this cause social breakdown or a more free and equal future? The following chapter examines gender from different perspectives. The viewpoint authors present varying opinions on what gender is and what it should be.

> *"The idea of having only two scripts for more than 7 billion people living in this planet is hilarious and outdated."*

Having Only Two Genders Is Ridiculous

Avinaba Dutta

In the following viewpoint, Avinaba Dutta argues that gender is a social construct. He notes that people are typically assigned gender at birth, based on their genitals. Society then pressures people to behave in line with society's ideas of what is masculine or feminine. He calls this idea outdated, because it allows for only two scripts that people can follow. Instead, he suggests people should navigate their own ideas of gender. Avinaba Dutta works at the University of Ottawa and sometimes writes about India and the history of LGBTQ rights.

As you read, consider the following questions:

1. How does the author define a "social construct"?
2. How can we tell that gender is not directly connected to biology, according to the viewpoint?
3. Why was the idea of gender created, according to the author?

"We've All Heard 'Gender Is A Social Construct,' But What Does That Really Mean?" by Avinaba Dutta, YKA Media Pvt. Ltd. Reprinted by permission.

A few weeks ago, my mom, after having a haircut, had an announcement to make—next time she would like to have a "boys" cut. My nephew had a series of questions. "Didu, what is boys' cut?" The 8-year-old asked my mom. And once she had explained to him what 'boys' cut' really is, he asked "But, didu, you are a girl and girls do not cut their hair like boys do." His view of gender segregation didn't really surprise me, because he's seen my family asking me why I had pierced my ears like "girls" do.

How many of us ever wondered where all these stereotypes had come from? The answer lies in "gender," or more precisely, the social construction of gender.

How Gender Is Socially Constructed

A social construct is a concept which cannot exist independently in the natural world and everything we know or perceive as reality, is entirely, or at least partially, socially situated. For an instance, "money" is a socially constructed reality. The paper bills we use in India, i.e. Indian Rupee, are only worth as much as value as the Reserve Bank of India assigns to it. Without our practices of assigning values to those paper bills, can money exist independently in nature? The answer is no. And while being part of this socially constructed reality it will be pretty foolish of us if we go to El Tizoncito in Mexico City and pay in Indian Rupee after enjoying a yummy plate of steak or pulled pork tacos. This is because being part of the same social construct (money), Indians built few norms which are different than its Mexican counterpart.

But we must understand that by reminding everyone about how socially constructed a particular concept is, we cannot diminish the power of that concept. Neither does it make the concept an imaginary one. It only demonstrates that the existence of that particular concept depends upon our practices and cultures, and changes from one time-period and culture to another.

Most of these sociological theories of social constructionism apply to gender as well. However, while understanding the implications of a social construction theory of gender, it is also indispensable to keep "gender" separate from 'gender identity' and 'biological sex' of an individual.

Gender, as we know it, is predominantly defined (imposed) based on what external genitalia one is born with. The practice of looking at a baby's genitals and assigning a gender to them at their birth is later followed by an extensive training program based on only two available scripts, i.e. "boy" (man or masculinity) and "girl" (woman or femininity). We slowly learn which emotions we are supposed to express, which colours we should like, what kind of hobbies we are supposed to have, what toys to play with, what songs we should listen to, whether to like sports or not, whether to learn cooking or not. We also learn how to talk to each other, what body language to use, what occupations to pursue, what kind of wages we are expected to have, whom to fall in love with, whom to be sexually attracted to, and much more. Someone born with a penis is literally bombarded with toys like G. I. Joe action figures and cricket bats; they are always reminded that, unlike girls, "boys do not cry"; they will also be told to get married and "take care" of their wife and kids. And if someone seems to deviate from the script assigned to them, we try our best to "correct" them. We keep them on track with question and statements like, "Are you a boy?" "Do not act like a girl", "That makes you look like a girl", or "Are you homo?"

But Do We Need Scripts at All?

Gender is a social construct where behaviours or traits of two norms, i.e. "masculinity" and "femininity" differ drastically from one time-period and culture to another. For an instance, unlike traditional Indian culture, in Chinese culture girls are expected not to wear make-ups or any such ornaments. In Indian culture, drivers of a public transportation system are predominantly male, whereas in Western culture both males and females are hired for the same job. In non-Western cultures, boys, irrespective of their sexual orientation, are allowed to hold hands or hug, while in the West these acts of showing emotions are strictly prohibited until

GENDER IS REAL

Gender is a social construction.

Even if you take the most extreme biological determinist stance (which a lot of the "gender isn't a social construction" crowd take), you cannot deny the following:

- What it means to be a "woman" or "man" changes over time (often within the timeframe of a generation—ask your grandparents if you don't believe me).
- Further, right now, the traits associated with each of those roles are different in different parts of the world (watch a sitcom from another country if you don't believe me).

If our understanding of gender changes faster than our biology could possibly evolve, and currently exists in many forms around the world reflecting cultural differences, it's socially constructed. End of argument. That's what those two words, combined, mean.

And gender is real.

Just because something's a social construction doesn't mean it's not real (despite many fellow "social construction" folks saying so).

The famous example: money. Nobody would argue that there is any inherent value in the paper; we instead buy into the idea that it's valuable. Money is a social construction, and it's very, very real. It's life-or-death real (try living without it if you don't believe me). Ditto for gender.

Gender is one of the few ways we still allow (actually, encourage) systemic, identity-based discrimination and segregation. It's one of the fundamental ways we're taught to see the world, and the world is taught to see us. It's infused in our names and how we talk about others.

Now, is it based in biology? Influenced by? Completely unmoored from? That's a different argument, and one we can't get to until we stop conflating it with this one.

It's like arguing about the gold standard.

My take: gold's intrinsic value is misconstrued. Read into that whatever you'd like.

"Yes, Gender Is a Social Construction. No, That Doesn't Mean It's Not Real," by Sam Killermann, September 13, 2018.

they are between homosexual males—and even that is frowned on! The varied norm based on societal imposition reinforces the idea that gender is nothing but a social construct. Think about it for a moment—had gender been some sort of essence emerging from one's biological sex, it probably would have remained constant across space and time.

To understand the need for scripts, we need to comprehend the need for "gender" in the first place. "Gender" was created to build up a hierarchy solely based on power. But to give the hierarchy a more "natural" or "scientific" look, a few physical differences, like genitalia or secondary sexual characteristics, were adopted as the basic building block of the same. This made two distinct groups which are presumed to be essentially different. That's why we are asked to believe that femininity is weaker than masculinity. If someone is confused about how power structure plays its role in gender, please try to answer these few questions. How many men are comfortable in marrying women who are taller or more "masculine" than them? While females wear jeans and shirts, how many males are encouraged to wear skirts and sarees? Or why is society fine with masculine women but ridicules feminine men?

Pizza Rolls, Not Gender Roles!

A friend of mine from Netherlands once told me how tough it is for him to date a girl because of his "soft" nature which meant people perceived him as being gay.

Clearly, these two scripts are not a great fit for many of us, but still we manage to pass. We adapt and adjust in order to make those features of ourselves that do not fit the script look less conspicuous. But many cannot even think of fitting in. For example, a cisgender homosexual woman finds it tough to fit herself in one of the two scripts which expects her to get married to a person of the opposite sex. For a gender queer person, they are not even welcome to be a part of these two scripts.

Since the two scripts do not give importance to individuals' gender and sexual identities and the choices they want to make, they become a tool for oppression. But what happens if we start going around and deciding our own identity and our own positions in the hierarchy? The power hierarchy and the social construction of gender will fall apart. People will learn more about their gender identity, one of their core identities. We will also understand that sexual attraction is based on one's sexual orientation which is fluid for many. The idea of having only two scripts for more than 7 billion people living in this planet is hilarious and outdated. If "gender," the social construct, can adopt changes where individuals are allowed to navigate their own gender formation and locate their own spot on gender continuum, that will lead to a lot less dissonance and uncomfortable performances, not to mention the physical danger and stigma for those who don't adhere to the script to which they assigned.

> *"If being a man doesn't mean anything, why go through the work of taking on masculine traits?"*

Society Needs Gender Roles

John Hawkins

In the following viewpoint, John Hawkins claims that gender is not a social construct. He suggests that certain criteria are standard throughout time periods and cultures. In particular, the author claims that men do the dangerous and violent work. He suggests that weakening gender roles is bad for individuals and society. He envisions an extreme future where people might claim to be aliens or animals and insist others treat them as such. John Hawkins is a conservative blogger and columnist. He created a website called Right Wing News.

As you read, consider the following questions:

1. What does this author see as masculine values around the world?
2. What does this author see as feminine values around the world?
3. This author claims that eliminating social standards of gender is bad for society. What are his reasons?

"Sorry, Liberals, But Gender Is Not a 'Social Construct,'" by John Hawkins, Townhall.com, May 17, 2016. Reprinted by permission.

One of the most harmful and also false ideas that liberals have introduced to American culture is the idea that gender is nothing more than a "social construct." Put another way, there's no real difference between men and women; we just think there are differences because we accept illogical cultural norms that have been passed down through the years.

This is a "the moon is made out of green cheese" grade dumb concept; yet and still this idea undergirds liberal feminism. If a man can do it, then a woman can do it just as well, even if we're talking about the military, firemen or being a cop. It's the core concept that allows liberals to try to present transgenderism as a civil rights issue instead of a mental health issue. Undoubtedly, it's also part of the reason you see so many sad, lost, nearly androgynous young men these days. If being a man doesn't mean anything, why go through the work of taking on masculine traits?

The sleight of hand that liberals use to promote this obviously foolish idea is to point out that different cultures have different definitions of what constitutes manliness. To many Americans, enduring boot camp and becoming a soldier is a great way to prove your masculinity. To become a man in the Sateré-Mawé tribe, a boy must stick his hand in a glove full of venomous ants with incredibly painful bites and hold it there. On the Greek island of Kalymnos, manhood is proven via deep diving without equipment. Those men consider using diving equipment for safety to be effeminate.

You could be the epitome of manhood in America without ever allowing yourself to be bitten by venomous ants or a man's man in the Sateré-Mawé tribe without ever deep diving; so doesn't that mean gender is a social construct?

No, stupid.

As Jack Donovan has noted, "Strength, Courage, Mastery, and Honor are the alpha virtues of men all over the world." A hard-assed American drill sergeant might think it's dumb as dirt to stick your hand in a glove full of Bullet Ants, but I can guaran-damn-tee you he has a certain level of manly respect for a guy who's tough enough to do it.

In a Panic over Gender

Think gender is determined by patriarchal biological concepts like a chromosome? You'll never make it in sociology thinking that way.

Instead, the social sciences are slowly overturning concepts like genital and chromosomes and other science, and it is being replaced by self-identity. The criteria for determining gender now, say Laurel Westbrook, assistant professor of sociology at Grand Valley State, and Kristen Schilt, assistant professor of sociology at the University of Chicago, have changed and self-identity is paramount. Only sex-segregated spaces believe that biology determines gender, they conclude.

If that becomes policy, it means that every female record in sports is going to be overturned soon. And that isn't the only way women will be impacted in society. Right now, the sociologists argue, transgendered people are not allowed in female locker rooms or bathrooms or sports teams due to legacy understanding of gender as biological. Westbrook said as a result of these fears, transgender rights policies are often discarded or altered in ways that force transgender people to conform to normative ideas of gendered bodies in order to access public facilities and activities that fit their identities.

Moreover, there are no cultures anywhere where let's say someone like Justin Bieber would be considered manly while someone like John Wayne would be considered feminine. Similarly, there are no cultures like the fictitious Amazons where women do the fighting while the men hang back. In the early 1900s, explorer Ernest Shackleton needed volunteers for a South Pole expedition. He placed an advertisement that read like so in the London Times: "Men wanted for hazardous journey, small wages, bitter cold, long months of complete darkness, constant danger, safe return doubtful; honor and recognition in case of success." The following day, over 5000 men showed up to volunteer.

"We explore the criteria for determining who is a 'man' and who is a 'woman' in sex-segregated spaces," said Westbrook. "We are at an interesting point in the history of gender, where people are torn between valuing self-identity and believing that biology determines gender. Our study explores that change in the gender system."

They examined case studies involving public debates over the expansion of transgender employment rights, policies determining eligibility of transgender people for competitive sports, and proposals to remove the genital surgery requirement for a change of sex marker on birth certificates.

"Transgender equality has never been more visible as a key issue than it is today, and with the development of every new trans-supportive law or policy, there typically follows an outbreak of criticism," said Westbrook. "In our analysis, we find that these moments, which we term 'gender panics,' are the result of a clash between two competing cultural ideas about gender identity: a belief that gender is determined by biology versus a belief that a person's self-identity in terms of gender should be validated. These gender panics frequently result in a reshaping of the language of such policies so that they require extensive bodily changes before transgender individuals have access to particular rights."

"Gender Is Not Biological, Find Sociologists," Science 2.0, Ion Publications LLC, October 28, 2013.

Note that 5000 MEN showed up to volunteer. In no culture in the world would women ever be the majority of people showing up for something like that. Not today, not last year, not at any point in history. Yet, if gender really were merely social construct, we'd expect to see women making up the majority of warriors, hunters and the people doing backbreaking, dangerous jobs SOMEWHERE. Along the same lines, there's no culture where men do the majority of the child rearing. If gender is really just a random, illogical series of habits that civilizations pick up, then we SHOULD see a lot more overlap, but we don't—and we never will.

Part of this is based on the very real physical differences between men and women. Men are taller, bigger, have more muscle mass. In violent confrontations with men or in tasks that require great strength, very few women can hope to compete with even the average male. This is the same across all cultures and it has helped create different incentives for men and woman. Men have been and still are the ones who do dirty, dangerous and violent work. Men who are good at it are admired by other men and sought out by women. Equivalently, women are admired for their beauty and their feminine wiles. Again, this is something you'll find across all cultures which again shows you that gender is not a social construct. Instead it's an outgrowth of biological reality.

Convenient as it may be to liberalism to pretend that there's no difference between men and women, it's not good for society. We already have women being forced to share the bathroom with men who "feel" like women today. By the way, we're not likely to stop with that bit of silliness as this excerpt of my interview with Kathy Shaidle shows,

> Well, knowing that I collect these things so that I can write about them for Taki's, one of my old friends, a former blogger, said, "You'll like this." He e-mailed me this link to a Reddit room where everybody is chatting about these really weird people. Now we've all heard about a man trapped in a woman's body and so forth. Well, like I said earlier, there are people who feel the need to just keep pushing this sort of thing because the thrill of that has worn off socially. So there are people who believe that they're—say, black, disabled women in white male bodies or they believe that they are a planet or they believe that they are an alien. Now I met some of the "I think I'm an alien" people years ago.
>
> Hey, wait a second. What bathroom do those people get?
>
> Well, that's just it; they're going to have to put a little picture of like a gray alien on one of the doors or something like that. ... They all get together and some people think they're animals. And I don't mean furries which we've seen on CSI

or whatever. These are people who don't necessarily dress up as animals. They think, "I am a fox" and, "I know I look like a person, but I am a fox."

Yes, one day you may be threatened with prosecution by some liberal for refusing to refer to a woman who believes she's a fox by her animal name "Arf Arf." That's not a future any of us should want.

> "*How is it that a concept that's been accepted by biology and neuroscience for decades could be abruptly rejected by outsiders?*"

Science Separates Males and Females

Eric Sexton

In the following viewpoint, Eric Sexton examines sex and gender from a neuroscience perspective. Neuroscience is the study of the brain and nervous system. The author notes that in many areas, men and women have some overlap in abilities. However, biological sex does have a strong effect on brain chemistry and on physical and mental abilities. Overall, the author says, science supports separating people into male or female. Statistics show the bimodal distribution of biological sex. Bimodal distribution refers to a dataset that divides most of the data into two groups. The author suggests that people who claim biological sex is a social concept are denying science. Eric Sexton is a scientist and writer.

As you read, consider the following questions:

1. What is the difference between biological sex and gender, according to the sources mentioned?
2. The author lists many statistics. How do these show ways that biological men and women overlap or differ for various traits?
3. Does biological sex influence people's brains, according to the author?

A few months ago a *Scientific American* editorial claimed that "most of us are biological hybrids on a male—female continuum". The editorial managed to upset the scientific community. I first heard of it when Steven Pinker, a cognitive scientist at Harvard, tweeted a link to a sound rebuttal of the editorial by University of Chicago biologist Jerry Coyne. This bit of controversy piqued my interest. Fast forward to this past week when I heard "trans studies" professor Nicholas Matte flat out claim that biological sex doesn't exist. It appears the idea that biological sex either doesn't exist or is a social construct is becoming more popular. So does it exist? Is it simply a "social construct"?

Biological Sex vs Gender

First, a distinction must be made between biological sex and gender. According to the *APA Dictionary of Psychology* sex is:

> The traits that distinguish between males and females. Sex refers especially to physical and biological traits, whereas GENDER refers especially to social or cultural traits, although the distinction between the two terms is not regularly observed.

Or according to "Guidelines for psychological practice with lesbian, gay, and bisexual clients,"

> Sex refers to a person's biological status and is typically categorized as male, female, or intersex (i.e., atypical combinations of features that usually distinguish male from female). There are a number

of indicators of biological sex, including sex chromosomes, gonads, internal reproductive organs, and external genitalia.

And one more for good measure. Planned Parenthood (American Federal Government) says:

> Sex is a label—male or female—that you're assigned by a doctor at birth based on the genitals you're born with and the chromosomes you have. It goes on your birth certificate.

So just to emphasize, I'm discussing biological sex and not gender.

What Is Biological Sex?

The fact is that the overwhelming majority of human beings are born with either an XY or XX chromosomal constitution. About half the human population is born with an XY chromosomal constitution and the other half is born with XX. This is what's referred to as a bimodal distribution. Of course, intersex people are an exception. Intersex births account for roughly 2% of the human population. So roughly 98% of all humans are born with one of these two chromosomal constitutions.

But to simplify biological sex to the presence or absence of a Y chromosome is still incorrect. This would imply that there is a strict "binary" wherein biological males exhibit a set of traits and biological females exhibit another unique set of traits with zero overlap. There are however, varying degrees of differences on average between males and females. To explain this I will quote psychologist Dr. David P Schmitt at length:

> One way to clarify discussions about differences in group averages is to put a specific number to them. Psychologists often use a precise number to express the size of sex differences, referred to as an "effect size," with the most common usage being the d statistic. A positive d value typically indicates that men are higher on a particular attribute; a negative value indicates that women are higher. The size of the d value establishes exactly how big the average sex difference is.

A d value near zero means that the sex difference is trivial. Once a d value reaches +/- 0.20, psychologists take notice. A d value of -0.20, for instance, indicates that 58 percent of women are higher than the average man on a psychological trait. These are considered "small" effect sizes. Sex differences in interpersonal trust, conformity, and general verbal ability reside in this range.

A d value of +0.50 is considered "moderate" and indicates that 69 percent of men are higher than the average woman on a particular attribute. Sex differences in spatial rotation skills, certain mathematics abilities (3-dimensional geometry and calculus), and task-oriented leadership (focusing on accomplishing a group goal rather than maintaining harmony within the group) reside within this size range.

A d value of -0.80 is considered "large" and indicates that 79 percent of women are higher than the average man. Sex differences in tender-mindedness, being interested more in people than in things, and lack of interest in casual sex reside in this size range.

Larger d values are less common in psychology, but a value of +1.00 indicates that 84 percent of men are higher than the average woman. Sex differences of this magnitude include differences in height, in expressing interest in engineering as an occupation, and in absence of sexual disgust (such as not feeling grossed out when hearing the neighbors having sex).

A d value of +2.00 indicates that 98 percent of men are higher than the average woman in a trait, about as close as researchers can get to finding a truly dimorphic difference. Sex differences in throwing ability, grip strength, and voice pitch are in this range.

No matter how big or small a sex difference, there is almost always significant overlap across distributions of men and women. Some women are able to throw farther than some men. Psychological sex differences are about group distributions, not dichotomous binaries of all men versus all women.

Reviewing the Data

In fact the sexual differences between men and women are increasingly supported across disciplines. As Schmitt notes:

> Converging lines of empirical evidence—from developmental neuroscience, medical genetics, evolutionary biology, cross-cultural psychology, and new studies of transsexuality—along with our evolutionary heritage, all point to the same conclusion: There are psychological differences between men and women.

And indeed the evidence is rather overwhelming. A quick review of the literature shows that in the hard sciences (e.g. biology, neuroscience) as well as cognitive science the question isn't whether biological sex exists, but rather the how much biological sex influences our behavior. For instance, it has been demonstrated that prenatal androgen exposure has serious impact on behavior including toy preferences, occupational choice, and even gender development (also see here). Additional studies have shown males are biologically predisposed to higher rates of autism and women are more likely to suffer from depression, in part due to biological causes.

And the psychology literature paints a similar picture: biological females generally score higher in neuroticism (No, not that neuroticism. I mean technically.) and agreeableness (again, a technical term). Additional studies further support these findings.

Neuroscientific literature not only supports the existence of biological sex, but entirely accepts its existence and develops studies to understand its impact. Male and female brains are shown to differ in connectivity, percentage of gray matter, memory, and brain aging. In fact, neuroscience has more clearly delineated the impact of biological sex than most other fields. An article in Nature Reviews Neuroscience even went so far as to say that:

> Research into sex influences is mandatory to fully understand a host of brain disorders with sex differences in their incidence and/or nature. The striking quantity and diversity of sex-related influences on brain function indicate that the still widespread

assumption that sex influences are negligible cannot be justified, and probably retards progress in our field.

The Origins of Biological Sex Denial

The question that arises is why—despite such compelling evidence of the impact and importance of biological sex—do some social scientists continue to reject its importance (or even existence!)? That is to say, why is the existence of biological sex a non-issue in the hard sciences but conspicuously under scrutiny elsewhere in academia? At least in part, the rejection of biological sex seems to stem from disciplines which either reject objective science outright or suffer from systemic replication problems. The latter group is made up of fields like social psychology where "findings were less than half as likely to replicate as findings in cognitive psychology." The former group primarily consists of fields like women's studies, gender studies, ethnic studies, and trans studies. In every case it's likely that a belief in the so called "blank slate" theory is motivating the researchers within the social sciences. This theory denies that evolution affected the development of the human mind. Which is a rather incredible belief when you really think about it. Not surprisingly, Harvard cognitive scientist Steven Pinker wrote a popular book debunking the blank slate in 2002. In it he details how biology and the hard sciences have rejected the theory for decades, but somehow the idea has managed to stay alive in the social sciences. Funny how the more things change, the more they stay the same, eh?

So clearly biological sex exists. Some activists (and social scientists in the above disciplines) reject the distinction of biological sex because it "alienates" or "marginalizes" the intersex community. However, the terminology of "male" and "female" is used to represent the bimodal distribution of biological sex. It's a useful term. To reject it simply because it "marginalizes" is ludicrous. Here's why: Humans are also biologically categorized as binocular animals. We typically have two eyes. Doesn't that "marginalize" humans born with Cyclopia, a birth defect which produces one eye? Humans are also considered bipedal. That term necessarily "marginalizes" humans born with one leg. So on and so forth. When approached logically the claim that "biological sex" marginalizes becomes a statement of obvious fact. Language categorizes and thus marginalizes, by definition. The fight against biological sex isn't just a revolt against scientific consensus. It's a revolt against language itself.

So is biological sex a social construct? Well sure, in the same way that the words "dog" or "cat" are social constructs. Language itself is a social construct. This statement of obvious fact doesn't tell us very much, however. What people typically mean when they claim that "biological sex is a social construct" is that biological sex is entirely divorced from biology. This claim is false.

Final Thoughts

I started writing this out of pure scientific curiosity. But after reviewing the literature across disciplines it became incredibly clear that certain fields of study must ask themselves why it is that they're in disagreement with the hard sciences. How is it that a concept that's been accepted by biology and neuroscience for decades could be abruptly rejected by outsiders? And what are the consequences of fields of study which often openly deny the scientific method? Could it be that rejecting the scientific method becomes a useful tool when science doesn't agree with your ideology?

In the end I can't stop someone from insisting that biological sex is a social construct or denying its existence altogether. After all, all one needs to do is look up a women's studies journal and find some "autobiographical" essay demonstrating that objective facts are a tool of the patriarchy and boom, game over. The real question become what is knowledge and which sources of knowledge do you trust? Ultimately that decision is up to the individual. And if an individual chooses to deny objective scientific truth, that's fine. I just wish they would stop hiding behind science while doing so.

| *"Usually we think of gender as natural and biological, but it's not..."*

Gender Is Bad for Mental Health

Tara Culp-Ressler

The following viewpoint looks at gender research from the perspective of sociology. Sociology is the study of human social relationships and culture. Tara Culp-Ressler discusses a study of teenagers conducted in Portugal. A researcher observed and interviewed teenagers over the course of three months. She observed many signs that the teens were submitting to social pressure based on their gender. She concluded that these behaviors were physically and emotionally dangerous. At the end of the study, the teens were surprised to learn that most of them did not want to follow strict gender roles. Tara Culp-Ressler is the managing editor of ThinkProgress, a news website with a progressive viewpoint. She was previously a health reporter and editor.

As you read, consider the following questions:

1. How did the researcher described in this article conduct her study?
2. What unhealthy behaviors did she observe?
3. How did the teenagers respond when they learned the results of the study?

"Forcing Kids to Stick to Gender Roles Can Actually Be Harmful to Their Health," by Tara Culp-Ressler, ThinkProgress, August 7, 2014. Reprinted by permission.

Raising children in societies that adhere to rigid gender roles, with fixed ideas about what should be considered "masculine" and "feminine," can actually be detrimental to their physical and mental health, according to a study that observed 14-year-olds' interactions over a three month period.

"Usually we think of gender as natural and biological, but it's not… We actually construct it in ways that have problematic and largely unacknowledged health risks," lead researcher Maria do Mar Pereira, the deputy director for the University of Warwick's Centre for the Study of Women and Gender, explained in an interview with ThinkProgress.

Pereira drew her conclusions after being embedded in a class of teenagers in Lisbon, Portugal. The kids in the study knew they were being observed by Pereira—who participated in all aspects of their everyday lives, including attending classes, eating lunch in the cafeteria, playing on the playground, and joining them on trips to the mall after school—but they didn't know her specific area of focus. In addition to her one-on-one interviews with each teen, her observations allowed her to track the ways they interacted with their ideas about masculinity and femininity.

Pereira observed both boys and girls regulating their behavior in potentially harmful ways in order to adhere to gender norms. For instance, even girls who enjoyed sports often avoided physical activity at school because they assumed it wouldn't be a feminine thing to do, they worried they might look unattractive while running, or they were mocked by their male peers for not being good enough. The girls also put themselves on diets because they believed desirable women have to be skinny.

"All of the girls were within very healthy weights, but they were all restricting their intake of food in some way. So what we're really talking about here is 14-year-old girls, whose bodies are changing and developing, depriving themselves at every meal," Pereira said. "In the extreme, that can lead to things like eating disorders. But even for the women who don't reach the extreme, it can be very unhealthy for them."

Meanwhile, the male participants in the study all faced intense pressure to demonstrate the extent of their manliness, which led to what Pereira calls "everyday low-level violence": slapping and hitting each other, as well as inflicting pain on other boys' genitals. They were encouraged to physically fight each other if they were ever mocked or offended. They felt like they had to drink unhealthy amounts of alcohol because that's what a man would do. And they were under certain mental health strains, too; struggling with anxiety about proving themselves and suppressing their feelings, all while lacking a strong emotional support system.

Ultimately, the study concluded, "this constant effort to manage one's everyday life in line with gender norms produces significant anxiety, insecurity, stress and low self-esteem for both boys and girls, and both for 'popular' young people and those who have lower status in school." The findings ended up forming the basis of a book, *Doing Gender in the Playground*, about negotiating gender roles in schools.

But it doesn't have to be this way. The teens who participated in the Lisbon study—including the kids who bullied others and the kids who were victims of bullying themselves—weren't happy about the gender roles they were expected to follow. In their one-on-one interviews, they all said they didn't actually like paying so much attention to the right "feminine" and "masculine" behaviors, and just assumed that's what they were supposed to do. When Pereira concluded her research and held a group meeting to explain her results to the kids, they were amazed to learn that everyone was on the same page about that.

"It was a revealing experience for them to be in that room and realize they were all performing and no one was happy about it," she recounted. Slowly, things started to change. Pereira acknowledges it's not like it was "suddenly paradise," but she noticed the kids stopped mocking their peers as much for falling outside the bounds of traditionally gendered behavior. Girls and boys started to become more integrated in athletic activities. There was less physical fighting. And some of the kids' parents even started calling Pereira to tell her about positive changes in their behavior.

Although Pereria's observations took place at a school in Lisbon, she believes her results have widespread implications for Western nations that are subject to similar cultural messages about gender. Indeed, previous research in British and American schools has reached many of the same conclusions as her study. Sociologists agree that children "learn gender" from being subjected to society's expectations, even though pressuring kids to conform to those rigid roles can end up having serious mental health consequences for the children whose parents try to over-correct their behavior. There are countless examples of schools becoming environments where gender stereotypes are strictly policed and kids are even sent home for wearing the "wrong" type of clothing.

The Lisbon findings could also give people hope about the possibility of creating a different kind of approach to these issues. It's important to remember that teens are still shaping their attitudes about what it means to be a man or a woman.

"Sometimes adults think it's impossible to change gender norms because they're already so deeply entrenched. But they're much more entrenched in adults than they are in young people," Pereira pointed out. "It's actually fairly easy to reach young people if you create opportunities for discussion, if you get them to think about their own experiences."

| *"They are challenging the idea that men must dress a certain way, and women another."*

Young People Don't Need Old Gender Roles

Lidia Jean Kott

In the following viewpoint Lidia Jean Kott explores the views millennials (people born roughly between 1982 and 2004) have on gender. The report suggests that this generation is changing their views on gender. Many find traditional gender roles limiting. They're more willing to explore fashion across gender standards. Some may find a new look that suits them. Others may vary their fashion from day to day. Even those who still follow traditional feminine or masculine fashion may be more open-minded about what is acceptable for other people. Lidia Jean Kott is a journalist and former radio news producer.

As you read, consider the following questions:

1. Do the majority of millennials feel that gender defines a person strongly?
2. Do the majority of millennials still dress according to traditional gender roles?
3. How can "queer" differ from "gay," as suggested in this viewpoint?

Cameron Finucane, a burly, 26-year-old technology consultant in Ithaca, N.Y., started painting his nails a few months ago. He has just started dating Emily Coon, a 24-year-old writer who has sworn off nail polish.

Finucane and Coon, as well as many other millennials, say they find traditional notions of gender too confining, even ill-fitting. They are challenging the idea that men must dress a certain way, and women another. And they are rewriting the rules and refashioning clothes so that they can dress and accessorize in whatever way feels right to them.

More than two-thirds of people ages 14 to 34 agree that gender does not have to define a person in the way that it used to, according to a 2013 study conducted by the Intelligence Group, a consumer insights company. And 6 in 10 say that men and women do not need to conform to traditional gender roles or behaviors anymore.

Finucane always liked colors, he says. And one day, while watching his friend paint her nails, he decided he wanted to try, too. Nowadays, he almost always has his nails painted. He's done blue, yellow, pink. Finucane, who works with computers, even painted his nails all the colors of the inks used in color printing, which mix together to make most of the colors we see.

Coon thinks it's great that Finucane paints his nails. But she doesn't like it on herself. It makes her feel uncomfortable, "like if someone were forced to dress up in drag if they didn't want to," she says.

Self-Expression and Suits

Caitlin Ryan, a clinical social worker at San Francisco State University who studies sexual orientation and gender identity in youth, says many millennials, like Coon and Finucane, are defying gender expectations.

"This generation views gender as a mark of self-expression—they view it as a way of displaying their full sense of self," she says.

For example, Rae Tutera, who will appear in an upcoming documentary produced by Lena Dunham about gender nonconformity in fashion, says that the first time she felt like herself was in a men's suit.

Tutera, 29, says she is "on the masculine side of the gender spectrum." She has short hair and light freckles. While at a sandwich shop near her house in Brooklyn, she turned her back each time she took a bite out of her egg sandwich in case it got messy.

Tutera bought her first suit after she was invited to a formal New Year's Eve party five years ago.

"Sometimes you have to act braver than you feel," she says, remembering what it felt like to enter a fancy men's suit store in Manhattan.

Tutera has worn men's clothing for most of her life. But before, she says, the clothes hid her. In that suit, made exactly to her measurements, Tutera realized she has the right to be visible.

Tutera searched for a tailoring company where she could learn to make suits for other people like her, and make the process better. She ended up at Bindle & Keep, a company based out of New York City, and became their official "queer clothier." "Queer" in this case doesn't just mean gay; it also refers to anyone who finds that traditional gender categories don't quite fit.

Three Suits, Lena Dunham's documentary, will follow three of Tutera's clients as they get fitted for their first suits. It'll be about "the unparalleled meaning" these suits have in their lives, says Tutera.

Finding a Voice

But for some millennials, expressing their gender in a way that feels right is less about finding one article of clothing, or a set style, and more about fluidity.

Greg David, a 24-year-old employee of the chain clothing store Urban Outfitters in Washington, D.C., says, "There's certain days for it," when asked if he thinks of himself as masculine.

On any given day he might wear a flowing silk shirt, pants so tight as to be almost leggings and maybe even a brooch.

David came out as gay in high school. But it wasn't until college, when he realized he could wear whatever he wanted to, no matter what gender it was designed for, that he felt like he came into his own.

"Dressing this way is how I found my voice," he says.

Gender-bending millennials such as David aren't exactly the norm, though, according to Suzanna Walters, director of the Women's, Gender and Sexuality Studies Program at Northeastern University. She says most millennials don't push gender boundaries.

"It's a real minority. And it gets played up in the media more than everyday life. The vast majority of people still obey gender roles," she says. "Just walk down the street."

Mostly, you'll see millennial women dressed femininely, and millennial men dressed masculinely.

But many even conventionally dressed millennials are considering the ways in which gender might be flexible.

"It's something people are playing with: ... What does it mean to act more masculine in the classroom? More feminine when listening?" says Alejandra Oliva, a 22-year-old student at Columbia University.

It's questions like these that the gender-bending set raises both out loud and through clothes and accessories. And they're questions anyone can think about, whether or not they feel comfortable in nail polish.

> *"The goal instead is to be the best damn person you can be regardless of what you have between your legs."*

The Future Is Gender Indifference

Will Penney

In the following viewpoint, Will Penney starts by asking what it means to be a man. He then suggests that is the wrong question. Instead, he claims, a person's roles are determined by their individual circumstances and preferences. He imagines an ideal future, where gender differences are irrelevant. To get there, people need to identify sexism in themselves and others and then work to change their words and thoughts. Will Penney writes about life, happiness, and relationships. The Good Men Project encourages conversations about what modern, enlightened masculinity might look like.

As you read, consider the following questions:

1. What does the viewpoint author mean by gender being "irrelevant" in the future?
2. How can we stop using gendered phrases, and why should we, according to the article?
3. Will people truly ignore gender in the future, according to the author?

"The Future Is Gender Indifference," by Will Penney, GoodMenProject.com, June 10, 2018. Reprinted by permission.

W hat does it currently mean, in 2018, to "be a man"? What are positive masculine traits we can emphasize in the future? What is the best way to define manhood now? How can we demonstrate the male gender positively to our children, to other peoples' children, and to adults who might as well be children?

If I may, I have a humble contribution to this ongoing conversation:

None of this really matters.

That sounds harsh, shortsighted, and maybe incredibly stupid, but let me explain.

When trying to create an ideal, less sexist future, trying to define ideal masculinity or femininity misses the point. Trying to find a future role for men or women misses the point. Trying to find different examples to set for boys and girls separately misses the damn point.

If we want actual gender equality, we can't keep dividing our views along gender lines. Instead, we must treat everyone equally.

The idea is therefore not to find a positive meaning in the phrase, "be a man." "Be a man" is not the goal. Beyond peeing standing up, and not feeding people with your nipples, your manhood is irrelevant.

The goal instead is to be the best damn person you can be regardless of what you have between your legs.

So let's break down all that this entails.

Jacks and Jills of All Trades

Roles have been and are still important. Somebody needs to manifest some cash to feed junior. Somebody needs to be there to make sure he doesn't walk into traffic. Somebody needs to make sure those reports go out in a timely manner. Somebody needs to be emotionally available for the crier in the family. Somebody needs to wash your a** (preferably yourself).

But more and more today, your roles are determined by you and your specific circumstances, and not society's blanket ideas about gender. Your roles are fluid now, and in the ideal future, they will be indistinguishable.

Your role in the modern world can change from provider to protector, to emotionally available counselor, to athlete, to chauffeur, to chef, to tutor, and that can all just be a Tuesday afternoon.

This is good. This is more equal.

But in order to both encourage more progress in this area, and to function better with these more fluid roles, we need to create more well-rounded people who can thrive in these roles. This means that we must address our weaknesses (both gender-driven, and otherwise) and become better people, and we must push others to do the same.

In terms of gender, this means that we must demand competence from everyone in all areas. Even if you're a testosterone-fueled, athletic boy, the ideal future still demands you be in touch emotionally, and calm the f*** down at dinner. Even if you're an eight-year-old girl, you have to carry some boxes on moving day, and learn that your looks aren't the most important part about you. More recently, we've discovered that even if you're a man with all the power in the world, you still can't show your d*** to people who don't want to see it.

The Move Towards Gender Indifference

This isn't to say that there aren't inherent biological differences between the genders outside of body parts and sizes, because of course there are.

But in an ideal future, these differences are irrelevant, because our expectations remain the same in the face of them. Our expectations aren't based on emotionally volatile, catty women, or emotionally incompetent, rowdy asshole men. They're based on everyone exuding strengths of both genders.

This also isn't to say we're seeking a genderless world. That will never happen. Humans are programmed to see people who look a certain way, and to categorize them as such. Men will always see women, and immediately register, "Oh that's a woman. That means she is x, y, and z." (This is especially exacerbated by the fact that x in that equation generally stands for, "a person I want to do the sex with.")

We can't hope to stop that. What we can control is what "x, y, and z" (or at least y and z) stand for in that example. We can change how we classify people. We can, through conditioning, change the way society views the genders to avoid using y and z to pre-assume personality traits, a status of women as being less than, or an obsession with shoes.

Setting Examples

Creating this world starts with identifying the part we take in sexism, and then the part that others take, and attempting to root it out. Once we fix our behavior, we can set a better example for others, and change the way others think about gender.

To get further in depth, this means we need an increased self-awareness about our own thought patterns. This can start by working backwards—by looking at the results of our thought patterns, and using that to clue us in on the thoughts themselves.

For example, we can update some gendered phrases—thereby examining the thought patterns behind them. Here are some of them:

Replace, "Boys will be boys" with "That boy is being an a******."

Replace "damsel in distress" with, "She's super f****** lazy, and whiny."

Replace, "Man up," with, "Stop sucking at life."

Replace, "She must be on her period," with "That girl is being an a******."

Replace, "You throw like a girl," with "You throw like someone who sucks at throwing."

We can also change our negative thought patterns into positive ones. This means we stop pushing anybody into activities based on gender. Stop telling boys to not cry. Stop telling girls they're pretty over and over until they believe that that is their value to the world.

Teach consent and sex-positivity to classrooms of boys and girls sitting next to each other. Give everyone equal responsibility, and equal input. Teach everyone, with complete equality, the all-important lesson of, "Don't be an a******."

The ideal future doesn't ignore genders, but it also doesn't celebrate them. It treats them like your cat treats you.

It exists with them. It acknowledges they're there, but lends them no importance. It looks at gender, and says, "Yeah, I see you. Who cares?"

We can create this world by being the cat. If we treat everyone the same, without gender in mind, then everyone will be encouraged to express emotions, everyone will be encouraged to be tough, and perhaps most importantly, no one will ever say the disgusting phrase, "Sack up," again.

Periodical and Internet Sources Bibliography

The following articles have been selected to supplement the diverse views presented in this chapter.

Anderson, Ryan T., "Biology Isn't Bigotry: Why Sex Matters in the Age of Gender Identity," Heritage Foundation, Feb 16, 2017. https://www.heritage.org/gender/commentary/biology-isnt-bigotry-why-sex-matters-the-age-gender-identity

Boucher, Samantha, "Gender Is More Than A Social Construct," Medium Corporation, Sep 11, 2016. https://medium.com/@wispinn/gender-isnt-just-a-social-construct-4f97751f4e70

"Challenging harmful gender norms," Unilever's global company, https://www.unilever.com/sustainable-living/enhancing-livelihoods/opportunities-for-women/Challenging-harmful-gender-norms/

Davis, Kathleen, "How Americans' Views On Gender Roles Are Hurting The Economy And Holding Us Back," *Fast Company*, June 28, 2016. https://www.fastcompany.com/3061253/whats-holding-the-us-back-from-achieving-gender-equality

Dutta, Avinaba, "We've All Heard 'Gender Is A Social Construct,' But What Does That Really Mean?" YKA Media Pvt. Ltd., Jul 2017. https://www.youthkiawaaz.com/2016/07/gender-binary-social-construct/

Hawkins, John, "Sorry, Liberals, But Gender Is Not a 'Social Construct'" Townhall.com/Salem Media, May 17, 2016. https://townhall.com/columnists/johnhawkins/2016/05/17/sorry-liberals-but-gender-is-not-a-social-construct-n2164148

Huisman, Julia Perla, "The Gender Gap: Changing roles in education and economy, love and marriage," *Northwest Indiana Times*, Nov 16, 2013. http://www.nwitimes.com/lifestyles/faith-and-values/the-gender-gap-changing-roles-in-education-and-economy-love/article_d228998d-d5e3-56af-bcb9-c8131ad68838.html

Jones, Amiee Jean, "The Negative Effects Of Gender Roles," Odyssey Media Group, Inc, Oct 7, 2016. https://www.theodysseyonline.com/negative-effects-gender-roles

Killermann, Sam, "Yes, gender is a social construction. No, that doesn't mean it's not real," It's Pronounced Metrosexual, Sep 13, 2018. https://www.itspronouncedmetrosexual.com/2018/09/yes-gender-is-a-social-construction-no-that-doesnt-mean-its-not-real/

Laughlin, Shepherd, "Gen Z goes beyond gender binaries in new Innovation Group data," J. Walter Thompson Intelligence, 11 Mar 2016. https://www.jwtintelligence.com/2016/03/gen-z-goes-beyond-gender-binaries-in-new-innovation-group-data/

News Staff, "Gender Is Not Biological, Find Sociologists," Science 2.0, Oct 28, 2013. https://www.science20.com/news_articles/gender_not_biological_find_sociologists-123256

Ostler, Blaire, "Postgenderism: Liberation from Homogenization," May 10, 2017. http://www.blaireostler.com/journal/2017/3/10/postgenderism-liberation-from-homogenization

SAGE, "How have gender stereotypes changed in the last 30 years?" Science X , Mar 9, 2016. https://phys.org/news/2016-03-gender-stereotypes-years.html

Sexton, Eric, "Biological Sex As A Social Construct," Medium Corporation. Nov 28, 2017. https://medium.com/@ES_4P/biological-sex-as-a-social-construct-b2583c222737

Weingarten, Elizabeth, "How To Shake Up Gender Norms," Time, Mar 31, 2015. http://amp.timeinc.net/time/3672297/future-gender-norms

Yenor, Scott, "Sex, Gender, and the Origin of the Culture Wars: An Intellectual History," Heritage Foundation, Jun 30, 2017. https://www.heritage.org/gender/report/sex-gender-and-the-origin-the-culture-wars-intellectual-history

OPPOSING
VIEWPOINTS®
SERIES

CHAPTER 2

What Is the Future of Femininity?

Chapter Preface

As attitudes about gender change, people debate what it means to be feminine. The scientific definition of female refers to a person bearing two X chromosomes. In the animal world, the female sex can produce eggs or give birth to offspring. "Feminine" refers to having the appearance or qualities traditionally associated with women. Feminine qualities have often included being physically weak, nurturing, and emotional.

Some people claim that women and men have largely achieved equality. That doesn't mean that life is perfect for both groups. Rather, each gender faces double standards that can cause harm. In this view, the goal is not simply to lift up women. Instead, it is to ensure truly equal treatment regardless of gender. This means dismantling stereotypes and systems that favor women.

Other people note that women still suffer from sexism around the world. Women face challenges that men face much less often. Rape, domestic violence, and sexual slavery affect far more women than men. In many countries, women have fewer legal rights. The media often portrays men in positions of power and women as weaker and less important. Women suffer because they are women. Therefore, they need political movements that support them. Feminism and the women's movement promote safety, equality, and opportunities for women. Yet if views on gender are changing, is it enough to support women? Is supporting women at odds with supporting trans people, queer people, or those who do not identify with any gender?

Some of this chapter's viewpoints imagine a future focused on humans, not men or women, where everyone is both feminine and masculine. Or, perhaps, no one is. The labels become meaningless and can be discarded. People can work together for shared goals based on humanity. Is this future possible? Will changing the words we use to describe ourselves help get us there? Authors explore what it means to be female and whether "feminine" is a word to be discarded or a rallying cry for the future.

> *"The same stereotyping affecting women more broadly is holding back the global economic growth and social progress that will come from increased gender equality and women's empowerment."*

Gender Equality Is 170 Years Away

Alan Jope

In the following viewpoint Alan Jope argues that gender equality is not only not progressing, but it is actually moving backward. Jope cites statistics from a report produced by the World Economic Forum that outlines the many things that are holding women back. This is detrimental for many reasons, including the fact that equality in the workplace would add $28 trillion to the global economy by 2025. The author proposes that policies must be enacted and that corporations and private industry can do their part as well to provide opportunities and change the cultural landscape to minimize stereotyping. Alan Jope is president of personal care at Unilever.

"Gender Equality Is 170 Years Away. We Cannot Wait That Long," by Alan Jope, World Economic Forum, January 19, 2017. Reprinted by permission.

As you read, consider the following questions:

1. By what percentage can an extra year of secondary education increase girls' income potential?
2. How is the "boys club" detrimental to women, according to the viewpoint?
3. What is Unilever's #unstereotype initiative intended to achieve?

E nabling women and girls represents the single biggest opportunity for human development and economic growth. Despite this and many organizations working to address the issues, according to the World Economic Forum's Global Gender Gap Report things have worsened during 2016 and economic gender equality will not be achieved for another 170 years. It is worrying that we are not making progress; unacceptable that we are moving backwards.

It is a well-quoted figure that equality for women in the labour force would add $28 trillion to the global economy by 2025. Providing girls with just one extra year of secondary education can increase their potential income by 15-25%. But outdated norms and gender stereotypes are impeding our own ability to achieve the systemic change required. The same stereotyping affecting women more broadly is holding back the global economic growth and social progress that will come from increased gender equality and women's empowerment.

Already, women are the world's most powerful consumers controlling 65% of consumer spending, with an economic impact growing year after year. It is estimated that their incomes will increase from $13 trillion to $18 trillion by 2018. In my job running Unilever's Personal Care business—manufacturing and selling everything from shampoos, soaps and skin creams to deodorants and toothpaste—women account for more than 70% of our sales. I need no convincing that women's development is worth investing in.

The Global Gender Gap Index: Top 10 Improved Countries

COUNTRY	PERCENTAGE IMPROVEMENT
Nicaragua	12%
Nepal	11%
Bolivia	11%
Slovenia	11%
France	10%
Cameroon	10%
Iceland	9%
Ecuador	8%
India	8%
Namibia	8%

Source: The Global Gender Gap Report 2016

Every day, 2 billion people use our products. I believe that we can use our scale and reach to effect a positive transformation by challenging the social norms and gender stereotypes that hold women back.

We have built partnerships with many stakeholders to help achieve this, for example between our skincare brand Pond's and the Vital Voices Partnership, to invest in women leaders who want to find solutions to socio-economic, environmental or human rights issues in their communities. We are also working with the Clinton Giustra Enterprise Partnership (CGEP) to train women entrepreneurs in developing countries and give them access to our distribution networks to help them and their communities to thrive. We are working with UN Women to create programmes to help secure women's safety in our tea value chain. Brands like Dove have paved the way by changing beauty stereotypes—Dove's Self Esteem Project was developed to ensure that the next generation grows up enjoying a positive relationship with the way they look—helping them to raise their self-esteem, realize their full potential and play an active role in society.

We have also invested in new research to better understand and help us tackle the stereotypes and cultural norms which lead to gender bias in the workplace. The findings, which we will present in more detail at the World Economic Forum Annual Meeting 2017 in Davos, are—if not altogether surprising—a stark reminder of how much needs to be addressed:

- Women are held back by traditional beliefs, with social norms continuing to push women into traditional roles. Women feel like they have to "get over" the bad behaviour of males in the workplace, rather than speak up (52% of global respondents). Men feel they must change their behaviour when women walk in the room (64%).
- Tradition takes hold. The impact of unequal sharing of housework and childcare is perceived differently: men don't see the challenges posed by cultural norms that women do. Only 36% of men see unequal sharing of housework and childcare as an issue.
- Both men and women share clearly defined and stereotypical views of what men and women are better at in the workplace. Launching a high-stakes project and heading massive organizational change are seen as men's domains; planning events for co-workers and building company culture are viewed as women's fortes.
- Men want to push gender equality forward, but are held back by their conceptions and fear of change. There is a belief that men don't really want women in senior leadership roles (75% of women, 59% of men agree that women are under-represented) suggesting a desire to sustain familiar masculine attitudes in business.
- Depressingly, the "boys club," like an old, outdated golf club, is still keeping women out of senior leadership roles. Of those surveyed, 72% globally agree that "men enjoy male camaraderie and bonding which is part of business" and that this contributes to "why women are largely under-represented in the C-Suite." Men aren't holding each other accountable:

55% highlight "men not challenging other men when they witness inappropriate behaviour" as one of the leading contributing factors to gender inequality in the workplace.

These largely unconscious biases and stereotypes are likely part of the reason behind the regression that—despite many well-meaning efforts—we have seen over the past year. To stop this backwards trend, and indeed to expedite progress towards gender parity, we must focus not only on policies, but also on the bias and negative stereotypes born of limiting social norms.

At Unilever, we have begun to assess our own role and are taking action in one of the areas in which we have the most impact: advertising. Through our research, we held a mirror up to ourselves and confirmed that advertising perpetuates unhelpful stereotypes:

- 61% of men globally agreed advertising sets unrealistic expectations and pressure on men as the "alpha male hero";
- 63% of women globally agreed "advertising sets unrealistic expectations and pressure on women");
- 70% of respondents globally agreed it would be a better world if today's children were not exposed to the gender stereotypes often portrayed in media and marketing.

In response to this, in June last year, we announced #unstereotype—a global ambition for all of our brands to advance advertising away from stereotypical portrayals of gender. We have only just started, but we are committed. And we are not only looking at our advertising—we have also made it a priority to promote opportunities for 5 million women by 2020 across our value chain: from our workplaces, through our supply chain and distribution networks; to our consumers, through our brands.

However, it would be foolish and arrogant of us to think that we can single-handedly change stereotypes or advance gender parity. By their very nature, norms and stereotypes are deeply entrenched. But this can be achieved, through sustained and collective action. Companies collaborating, or acting in concert, can exert a force greater than the sum of their parts—especially if they can also co-opt other organizations, governments and non-governmental bodies.

As business leaders, we must make use of joint platforms like the World Economic Forum's System Initiative on Gender, Education and Work to embed the advancement of women in strategic and business goals. We must sign up to the Women's Empowerment Principles, and support the work of influential groups, such as the UN High Level Panel on Women, to create powerful and lasting solutions.

We must not accept another year in which progress towards gender parity isn't made and we certainly cannot wait 170 years for women to have the role that they deserve.

| "Women are no longer destined to be reliant on a man for their livelihood and subsequently have freedom of choice in their relationships."

Women Have Overcome a Lot in Just 100 Years

Rosie Benson

In the following viewpoint, Rosie Benson argues that women have made tremendous gains in the last century. The author highlights advances in government, reproductive rights, the arts and sciences, and the workforce, noting trailblazers in these arenas. Yes there is still much work to be done, she cautions, and women must not take these advances for granted. Rosie Benson is a features writer for Boots UK Health & Beauty. She has written for Marie Claire UK *and the BBC.*

As you read, consider the following questions:

1. In what country do women make up almost 50 percent of MPs in government, according to the viewpoint?
2. How many women bosses of FTSE 100 companies are there, according to the author?
3. Why does it matter that women rule the music industry charts?

W omen have come a long way since 1917 when we couldn't vote, get legal protection from marital rape, or initiative divorce

Sadly, there are still many outdated and downright depressing anti-women laws in use around the world today—women in Saudi Arabia cannot drive or leave the house without a male guardian present. In conflict zones women often bear the brunt of brutality, and the current refugee crisis puts thousands of women and girls at risk of sex trafficking and exploitation. But there's no doubt we've come a long way.

Here are just some of the ways women's lives have changed in the last century:

We've Broken into Government

From the election of the first female MP Nancy Astor in 1919, women have been breaking new ground in government. We've had two female prime ministers, the first female Scottish minister, and there are currently more female MPs in parliament than ever before. Yet women still only make up 29% of all MPs. While this is far from an ideal 50/50 (or greater) scenario, it's encouraging that young girls can now see women like them in positions of power—anyone remember post-referendum, when for a brief period all of the major parties (bar one) were headed by a female MP? Encouragingly, organisations such as 50/50 parliament and the Women's Equality Party are working to address that imbalance. Iceland on the other hand are miles ahead of us—women make up almost 50% of their MPS, while in Rwanda men are in the minority with women outnumbering them by a 61/39% split in the lower house.

We've Taken Control of Our Reproductive Rights

British women gained access to the contraceptive pill in 1961 and to be honest, we've never looked back. For the first time ever women could finally be in control of their bodies, able to have children

THE FUTURE IS FEMININE

The future is not female. The future is feminine.

Genders are no longer serving us and it is time for a change. Instead of "woman" vs. "man," let's define ourselves by our interconnectedness, the shared forces that make us human.

We are all feminine and we are all masculine.

Imagine a world where you are born you, free to play with dolls and toy cars, wear blue and pink clothes, encouraged to cry and scream and express yourself without reason or validation or judgement.

What if our children can take the time to figure out who they are before they are defined by their gender. What if they can be strong and soft and unique and authentic in the classroom, in business and at home, surrounded by people who understand and support and love. Now let's create that world together.

The left side of the human brain is often regarded as the masculine side, as it is more logical, driven, analytical and fast paced. The left side of the brain is associated with aggression, physical strength, control and ego.

(and consequently give up work) as and when they liked. The 60s was also a defining decade for women's rights as abortion became legal in the UK. Later we gained access to the morning-after-pill and there are now many contraceptive options open to women—a huge change from 100 years ago when a woman's options were basically condoms, a diaphragm or the rhythm method.

We've Made It into the Workplace

Back in the 1900s a woman's employment options were limited— career orientated women could expect to be employed as a domestic servant, teacher, nurse or dressmaker. High-earning, traditionally "male" professions were simply not welcoming to women—the first woman to ever train as a doctor, Elizabeth

The right side of the brain is regarded as the feminine side, associated with creativity, inner-strength and intuition. Those who are right-brained tend to be artsy, sensitive, nurturing and easy-going.

All human beings have two sides of the brain, so we each possess both feminine and masculine qualities. In this way, gender is not mutually exclusive, meaning we all possess both feminine and masculine energies, as well as the emotional intelligence and insight to adjust as needed.

It is time to unlock the power of the feminine. After recognizing that we are all feminine and we are all masculine, we can see the current societal shift that is guiding us towards the feminine. For too long we have been taught to think of the feminine energy as the "weaker" energy. This mindset has led us to a state of political and environmental turmoil, as we are faced with aggressive leaders, industries and weather patterns that often make me scared for my future children's futures. In order to guarantee humanity's best chances of survival, we must harness the power of the femininity in all of us.

Feminism does not mean equal rights for men and women. Feminism is our collective freedom to be feminine.

The future is feminine.

"The Future is Feminine," by Jessica Assaf, Medium.com, March 15, 2018.

Garrett Anderson, faced huge obstacles attracting patients—even female ones. Because the majority of Victorian women relied on a husband for financial support, they were effectively trapped in their marriages. Unmarried women, or spinsters, were socially shunned and pitied. Today, women have broke into boardrooms, combat zones, businesses. Is our work done? No. There are currently just seven women bosses of FTSE 100 companies. BUT we have made big gains, and we will keep on making them.

We've Taken Control of Our Relationships

In the last 100 years divorce has lost its stigma, forced marriage has been outlawed (1973), and domestic violence and stalking—crimes overwhelmingly perpetrated against women—are finally taken seriously in both the law and media. Jill Saward, the first rape victim to waive her anonymity in 1986, bravely paved the way for an open discussion about rape and rape culture to happen in society—even if it has been a gradual and slow process. Women are no longer destined to be reliant on a man for their livelihood and subsequently have freedom of choice in their relationships. What matters now is that we don't allow Trump & Co. to turn back the clock.

We've Taken the Charts by Storm

Madonna, Adele, Beyonce, Mariah—need we say more? 20 years (20!) after the Spice Girls showed us what Girl Power was all about, women continue to rule the charts and are constantly pushing creative boundaries and inspiring us with their music. (We weren't the only ones who did a little victory dance when Taylor Swift became the first woman to win album of the year at the Grammy's twice, right? You slay Tay). Here's to inspiring the next generation of music superstars.

We've Gone to Infinity—and Beyond

Does the name Helen Sharman ring a bell with you? Well if it doesn't, it should. Helen was the first Briton (man or woman) to go into space, breaking new ground for women in science everywhere. In 2007 Peggy A. Whitson broke another glass ceiling when she became the first female commander of the International Space Station. This month Hidden Figures shines a spotlight on the vital work that three African American women did for NASA in the early years of the space race. It just shows that when we work together, there are no boundaries to what women can achieve.

And That's Not to Mention…

All the other great and bloody brilliant things that women have achieved in the last 100 years, for which there just isn't enough space to list. From Charlotte Bronte and George Eliot having to hide their identities, to J.K Rowling's millions. Or from zero women competing in the first modern Olympics to to Jessica Ennis-Hill and Serena Williams killing it in the sporting arena. To the women taking on Isis and protecting us on the front lines, we've come a long, long way in the last century. Here's to the next 100 years!

> "[W]omen footballers are asked to doll up and attend photoshoots to market their game, without compromising their claim to being athletes."

Women Face Double Standards

Nina Degele

In the following viewpoint, Nina Degele looks at gender in soccer (which is called football in most countries). In response to a statement made by the sport's commissioner, Degele argues that "The future of football is feminine" is irritatingly vague. It could mean more women will be playing football, which she sees as healthy progress. On the other hand, the statement could reflect practices that force female players to act traditionally feminine. The author explores the history of women playing amateur and professional football. She notes that double standards still exist. Being athletic merely reinforces masculine attributes in men. However, women players are expected to be both athletic and feminine, and these are often seen as opposing qualities. Nina Degele is professor of sociology and gender studies at the University of Frieburg.

"The Future Is Female—or Feminine?" by Nina Degele, Heinrich Boell Foundation, January 6, 2012. Reprinted by permission.

As you read, consider the following questions:

1. How did early football organizations control how women could play the game?
2. How does marketing affect women's football?
3. How are women players expected to prove that they are feminine as well as athletic?

T he future of football is feminine," announced FIFA boss, Joseph Blatter, fervently in 1995. Is this a hope or a threat? When it comes to femininity, things are not always cut and dry. It can mean that more girls and women will be visible in football than has been the case before—that would equate to a female kick, a natural state of affairs that is long overdue. At the same time, however, the DFB's slogan for advertising the FIFA Women's World Cup on home soil is "The beautiful side of 20ELEVEN"; the Mattel company recently began marketing Barbie dolls of Silvia Neid, the head coach of the German women's national team, and Birgit Prinz, the team's captain, while Slovakian supermodel Adriana Karembeu, in her capacity as women's football ambassador in France, heads a campaign promoting "Football in the Feminine". The type of femininity on display in these examples is more in line with the statement uttered by Blatter. To understand how little such developments contribute towards establishing a female kick, all you need to do is take a quick peek at the short history of women's football.

Brief Excursion into the History of Women's Football

A few decades after their British trailblazers, a group of female footballers organised themselves in 1930 and formed their very first football club, 1. Damen-Fußball-Club Frankfurt. Such "unfeminine" shenanigans were a thorn in the side of the DFB:

on 30.7.1955, it issued a ban prohibiting clubs from forming departments for women's football. The fact that the ban on women playing football was imposed shortly after the "Miracle of Berne", which saw the men's national team lift the World Cup in 1954, is no accident according to DFB Vice-President, Hannelore Ratzeburg. This was a time when men returning home at the end of the war were facing a collapse of their supposed natural male dominance in the light of the emergence of active, energetic women who had begun rebuilding Germany without them: further adding to their humiliation. Not least of all, the DFB and associations continued to be run by men who knew how to keep women at arm's length—although that did not prevent women from playing the game. 1970 saw the end of the ban on women playing football, because the DFB feared that, with the impending threat of women forming their own football association, it would lose control over women. The price: women were forced to play with a smaller ball used by youth players and had to wear studless football boots; they were ordered to play shorter matches of just 30 minutes per half, with a six-month winter break imposed to allow them to rest. Internationals remained banned until 1982.

In the GDR, the first company sports teams for women were introduced in the 1960s; the first and only international was played in 1990. Women's football was never banned in the GDR, but since it was not an Olympic sport at that time, no funding was made available for it and women's football ranked behind youth football and youth development football on the prestige scale. The first championship was held in 1979, although the word 'championship' was not actually used, but 'Bestenermittlung', which equates to 'a series to determine the best of the best'. Matches played during the playoffs in Potsdam in 1984 lasted a mere twenty minutes per half. Today, this may all seem rather crass, but it served to keep those trying to infiltrate the male domain at bay. What does this mean for the future of women's football?

How Is Women's Football Perceived Today?

Siegfried Dietrich, manager and investor at 1.Frauen-Fußball-Club Frankfurt, openly champions the professionalisation of the sport, even though he does not believe it to be feasible given that the majority of the traditional clubs have amateur organisational structures. "The more professionally women's football can be organised, the better the brand can be marketed." (FR, 21.12.10) At the same time, he rates women's football as more hands-on and more technical. There is less power and money in the women's than the men's game, he says, adding that the sport is clean and fair and inspires families to attend matches together. This specific marketing of women's football as a family event and the commercialisation of hominess are moving it into the mainstream. It remains to be seen, however, whether or not such a strategy will end up branding the sport a conservative haven of family bliss and not giving it the enhanced status it seeks.

Media Demands Mean Being Professional and Glamorous in One

Such conventional modernisation is now being joined by a trend which first became apparent at the last Women's Football World Cup in 2007: the trend towards personalisation, as in the case of Fatmire Bajramaj, Birgit Prinz, Kim Kulig or Nadine Angerer. As personal brands, they are expected to reconcile a contradiction in terms that has been thoroughly etched into the public's perception for decades: football skills and femininity. Whilst men are totally oblivious to any contradiction between football and masculinity, women footballers are asked to doll up and attend photoshoots to market their game, without compromising their claim to being athletes. Outside of football, the business world has been fraught with this dilemma for somewhat longer. Here, too, women are contending with similarly mixed messages: be professional, but for God's sake don't lose your femininity. In this respect, Blatter may not be alone in thinking of revealing bikini bottoms or sexy-fitting football shirts when talking about the future of women's football being feminine; three-time world champion Birgit Prinz did exactly the same—though with a refreshingly different perspective: "We want to market our sport, not our bums." (STERN, 14.2.2004) So, let them finally get on with it.

| "*Some sex differences in work and family roles may always persist; but we should certainly continue to work toward more flexibility, freedom, and options for everyone.*"

Feminism Should Focus on Gender Equality

Cathy Young

In the following viewpoint, Cathy Young debates the current state of the patriarchy. Patriarchy is a system of government or society in which men hold the power. Some journalists and academics now claim that women have largely achieved equality. Others deny this point. The author argues that both women and men suffer from stereotypes and biases. She claims that double standards are as likely to be favorable to women as to men. Therefore, she says, the focus should not be on promoting women. Rather, we should work toward a society that treats all people equally. This would sometimes mean that society is harder on women than it is now. Cathy Young is a journalist primarily known for her writing about rape and feminism. RealClearPolitics covers news and policy issues.

"Yes, Patriarchy Is Dead; the Feminists Prove It," by Cathy Young, RealClearPolitics, September 23, 2013. Reprinted by permission.

As you read, consider the following questions:

1. Why do some people believe that the patriarchy is dead?
2. If patriarchy isn't the problem, what is, according to Hanna Rosin?
3. Why does the viewpoint author say that feminism should be reinvented as a gender equity movement?

When writer Hanna Rosin recently published an article on Slate.com stating that "the patriarchy is dead," much of the feminist response amounted to "burn the heretic!" New Republic editor and blogger Nora Caplan-Bricker accused Rosin of "mansplaining"—the femosphere's pejorative term for supposedly obtuse and arrogant male arguments on gender, apparently now also applied to female dissent—and being the patriarchy's unwitting tool. San Jose State University philosophy professor Janet Stemwedel tweeted her gloating over Rosin's Wikipedia page being vandalized to read, for a brief time, "Hanna Rosin (born 1970) is a terrible human being."

Ironically, the feminist tendency to shoot the bringer of good news was the very topic of Rosin's essay, adapted from the new epilogue to the paperback edition of her book "The End of Men"— which, despite its title, is more about female ascendance than male decline. Rosin noted with bemusement that rebuttals to her report on women's rising fortunes were greeted with palpable relief—not by male chauvinists but by feminists. (It isn't just Rosin: When a recent study demonstrated that female political candidates are not judged more negatively than male ones, not even for their looks and dress, feminists reacted with either silence or sniping.)

So where is this dreaded American patriarchy Rosin is covering up? Some critiques of her argument boil down to "it's only affluent white women who are doing well" (and poor minority men are presumably basking in privilege). A gentleman critic, fellow Slate.com author Matthew Yglesias, cites men's numerical dominance in corporate America—as if Rosin might be unaware of these statistics. (One figure he omits: Women control 60 percent of the wealth in the United States.) But mostly, Rosin's detractors focus on women's abuse by men and on pervasive cultural biases against women, from beauty pressures to so-called "slut-shaming." Patriarchy, says Caplan-Bricker, is "living in a society where both women and men save their harshest judgment for women."

Do they, though? Such nebulous statements are nearly impossible to prove or disprove. Actually, researchers such as feminist social psychologist Alice Eagly of Northwestern University have consistently found that both sexes tend to view women more positively than men. Sure, this pro-female bias has its flip side: Women's perceived "niceness" may cause them to be seen as less fit for leadership and to be penalized for not being nice. But crude generalizations about misogyny bear little relation to real life in modern Western society.

Gender-based biases are not a one-way street. If women are still stigmatized more for sleeping around, men are stigmatized more for not having enough sex—even by some feminists whose choice insult for sexist men is to imply sexual deprivation. Women may experience more disapproval for delegating child care; men, for failing to be providers. We can endlessly debate whether these norms are rooted in nature or culture and whether they are valuable or harmful (or some mix of both). The fact remains that such double standards are not only perpetuated by men and women alike but, in this day and age, at least as likely to be favorable to women as to men.

It's really not that hard to find instances in which men are judged more harshly than women. Last May, after Arizona woman Jodi Arias was convicted in the brutal murder of her ex-boyfriend, jurors deadlocked on the death sentence because some saw mitigation in her alleged mental and verbal abuse by her victim—despite evidence that Arias was a habitual stalker. Around the same time, when novelist James Lasdun published a book about his nightmarish experience of being cyber-stalked by a former creative writing student whose romantic overtures he had rejected, a review in The *New Yorker* chided him for failing to admit his attraction to the woman and his role in leading her on. Reverse the genders in either case, and there would be howls of outrage about "victim-blaming." (Both incidents are also reminders that women aren't the only victims of abuse and violence from the opposite sex.)

Ultimately, the examples of patriarchy at work offered in responses to Rosin prove her point. They consist of complex issues oversimplified into a war on women (such as proposed abortion limits, which women in some cases support more than men); outlandish exaggerations (women can't walk down the street without getting groped or catcalled); culturally marginal irrelevancies (some ultraconservative Catholic group advising against college education for women); or grievances so petty that it's hard to tell if they're satirical or serious. A list of "39 Things We'll Miss About Patriarchy, Which Is Dead" on New York magazine's website included "vibrators shaped like cupcakes," public restroom lines, and men hogging space on public transit. And several writers mentioned "Titstare"—an incident both trivial and revealing of strong societal disapproval of even mild sexism.

"Titstare," if you were lucky enough to miss the brouhaha, was a joke presentation by two Australian techies at the TechCrunch Disrupt "hackathon" earlier this month: a smartphone app for men to share photos of themselves ogling women's breasts. While the 60-second demo featured nothing more graphic than a couple of cleavage shots, it was certainly a bad joke—though arguably mostly at the expense of leering men (complete with a comic-style image of a man getting punched by a woman). But none of the commentators who cited this juvenile stunt as evidence of rampant misogyny saw fit to acknowledge that it was promptly followed by apologies from the two TechCrunch runners—one of them a woman, as were two of the five hackathon judges—and a pledge to pre-screen submissions more carefully at future events. If this ends up on a list of patriarchal offenses, one may start wondering if feminism has any real battles to fight.

Not Feminine but Human

I support anyone who identifies as a woman or was born a female, men who support women, males who support females, transpeople. I just love people, okay? It feels so ridiculous to me that anyone could not support any and everyone.

So, when I say I am not a feminist, it is not a description of my beliefs or actions—but a gripe with the words themselves.

"Feminist."

"Feminine."

This is why I say the future is undoubtedly female, but I hope it's not feminine. Not because I have any qualms with anyone being themselves in any way they want to be. If you want to get your hair done, do your nails, dance ballet, watch rom coms—do it! Absolutely do it. I do this stuff all the time.

But, I don't like that we call these things "feminine."

These are just things that some humans like to do. And, by labeling certain actions or attributes as "masculine" or "feminine," I honestly think we are holding ourselves back.

The way we use the word "masculine" in our culture tends to mean a few things: powerful, strong, sharply edged, pushy, stubborn, hard-working, emotionless at times, logical, not particularly nurturing.

The way we use the word "feminine" usually means: soft, quieter, more sensual, timid at times, emotional, nurturing, caring, loving.

When we use words that relate to gender identity to describe these traits, we're holding up age-old stereotypes for both men and women, not to mention what we're doing for everyone who doesn't fall within the binary gender paradigm at all.

The truth is these are human traits—whether male, female, transgender, or elsewhere on the spectrum. And, as much as we are still operating under the false belief that some of these traits are seen more in men and others more in women, I think we can trace a lot of that back to the simple use of language.

If we were to change the language, would we change the way we see men, women, and gender non-conforming people? Could we change the way men and women, at least, "traditionally" behave?

I think so.

"The Future Is Female, but (I Hope) Not Feminine," by Natalie Grigson, Waylon H. Lewis Enterprises, August 15, 2017.

Which, actually, isn't quite what Rosin was saying. When we spoke a few days after the publication of her article, she stressed that problems do exist—but focusing on "patriarchy" as "an enemy we can take down" is a counterproductive distraction from the real issues. Foremost among those is the career-family conundrum. Take the progress of women in the tech industry: For all the handwringing about Titstare as a symptom of the sexism holding them back, the evidence suggests that it's hardly the main obstacle. In one study, women with advanced degrees in science, technology and engineering were 25 percent less likely than men to work in their field if they were married and raising children—but there was no gender gap for the single and childless.

Some sex differences in work and family roles may always persist; but we should certainly continue to work toward more flexibility, freedom, and options for everyone. Rosin believes these goals should be redefined as care-giving issues for both sexes rather than "women's issues," and here she is certainly on the right track, even if her favored solutions are probably more government-oriented than mine would be.

More broadly, I am convinced that if feminism is to have a positive future, it must reinvent itself as a gender equity movement advocating for both sexes and against all sexism. Focusing solely on female disadvantage was perfectly understandable when, whatever paternalistic benefits women might have enjoyed and whatever burdens men might have suffered, women were the ones lacking the basic rights of adult citizens. But today, there is simply no moral or rational justification for any fair-minded feminist to ignore (for instance) the more lenient treatment of female offenders in the justice system or the anti-father biases in family courts. The concept of feminism as equality of the sexes is increasingly on a collision course with feminism as a movement championing women.

In its present form—as a secular cult that should call itself the Sisters of Perpetual Grievance—feminism is far more a part of the problem than part of the solution. It clings to women's wrongs and turns women's rights into narcissistic entitlement. It is far too easily prone to bashing men while painting women as insultingly helpless and downplaying their human capacity for cruelty. (The notion that abuse and dominance would not exist without patriarchy is not only naively utopian but utterly sexist.) It is also deeply irrelevant to most women, only 5 percent of whom consider themselves "strong feminists," even though 82 percent believe that men and women should be social, political, and economic equals.

Of course the patriarchy—at least here in the West—is dead. Whether feminism deserves to survive it is up to the feminists.

> "*I often vacillate between boredom and continued frustration at the narrow focuses of the wider feminist movement.*"

The Feminist Movement Has Failed to Be Inclusive

Lola Okolosie

In the following viewpoint Lola Okolosie reacts to the same article by Hanna Rosin as the author of the previous viewpoint. However, as a black feminist, Okolosie has a different take on Rosin's argument. While she disagrees that women are the dominant force in society, she agrees that it is "elite feminists"—generally educated, white, middle class women—who stand to benefit from any power wrested from men. Okolosie notes that women on the margins are not included in the wider feminist movement and that Rosin completely misses this fact when claiming the patriarchy is dead. Lola Okolosie is a teacher and writer whose columns for the Guardian *explore race, feminism, and education.*

As you read, consider the following questions:

1. Why did Hanna Rosin assert that men are "the aggrieved sex"?
2. What examples does the author use to prove that Rosin is wrong about women being the dominant force in society?
3. What percentage of single parents are at risk of poverty?

A uthor Hanna Rosin last week asked us to gather in close and listen to her glib explanation of what she considered a little known reality—"patriarchy is dead." Rosin isn't one for pulling her punches and, I am sure, relished the criticisms that followed her central argument: that men are no longer "dominant"; in fact, they are "the aggrieved sex."

Putting aside for the moment the fact that Rosin has an incomplete view of patriarchy—it isn't solely about male economic power and influence—she argues that it is women who have brought about this demise of men. Her messianic mission to salvage a beleaguered western masculinity is based on this oft-touted argument, permutations of which I have had to endure many times: it is women who are to blame for taking men's work and thereby causing a crisis in masculinity that has led to all sorts—our appalling male suicide figures for one. And it is women who are to blame for rape and other gender-based violence.

Lest we be shocked by such a sweeping generalisation, Rosin makes clear that it is a particular kind of woman that has brought about "the end of men"—the well-educated and confident middle-class woman. And it is this aspect of what she had to say that resonated with my experience as a black feminist.

A "new era of female dominance" occupied by well-educated ambitious women, is Rosin's chief concern. Now, I do not believe that we live in an era where women are the dominant force within our society. Too many saddening statistics abound: from violence against women and girls to our higher likelihood of living in poverty to the gender pay gap and our low political representation—women are not dominant. It is true that progress is taking place, but to call it dominance is a stretch.

Nevertheless, Rosin's description of "elite feminists," a group she sees as benefitting from this "new era," is striking. These feminists are characterised by their strong print and online presence and their ability to contribute to dominant discourse. To these women, Rosin asks: "Why should they feel reassured to be told that men are still on top, that the old order had not been shaken?" And in writing that, Rosin touched upon a raw nerve. Unwittingly she echoes the words of Alice Walker, who argued that, "the problem with western feminists is that they take after their brothers and their fathers ... the struggle for many of these women has just been to get what the men have and share it with them."

Implicit in Rosin's question is the critique many LGBTQ, undocumented, working-class, disabled and black feminists level at the wider movement. If feminism is only about the concerns of the privileged few who now, ostensibly, wield the same type of power as their fathers and brothers, it leaves itself open to criticisms such as hers. I often vacillate between boredom and continued frustration at the narrow focuses of the wider feminist movement. The success of #SolidarityIsForWhiteWomen demonstrates how I am not the only one who feels this sustained sense of dissatisfaction.

However, Rosin's stance on what she considers the de facto death of patriarchy ignores the very women she believes she is speaking for, those that are marginalised. She suffers from the same blind-spot as the prominent white feminists she reserves much of her vitriol for. Her logic goes: feminists fight patriarchy, but patriarchy is dead because influential feminists and successful female graduates now have better prospects.

In this framework, the realities of existing under a male-dominated system closely aligned to a capitalist framework for LGBTQ/black/disabled/working-class/underclass/undocumented women can be neatly elided. She asserts that many single parents and working-class women, "yearn to bring back at least some aspects of patriarchy ... they long to have a man around who would pay the bills and take care of them and make a life for them in which they could work less."

Wanting another individual to help you manage the burden of your poverty is in effect lamenting the death of patriarchy. Indeed the struggle for single women with children to make ends meet becomes, for the purposes of her thesis, unrelated to our patriarchal society. Never mind that 52% of single parents are at an overall risk of poverty and that 92% of them are women, or that 22% of women as opposed to 14% of men have a persistent low income. Nope, patriarchy is dead and therefore not at fault.

I employ a flurry of statistics because some of Rosin's most dangerous remarks are delivered through the language of euphemism, rather than sobering, hard facts. For example, she writes that the "big picture" of life without patriarchy may not always be consistent with women's daily experiences; some women, she concedes, do have an "overbearing husband". This I take to be Rosin's code phrase for domestic violence. Overbearing sounds very far from the reality in which two women a week die at the hands of their partners or ex at the hands of their partners or ex. Nevertheless, if Rosin can lob some fair criticism at the feminist movement, it should be worried. It needs to ask itself if it truly reflects the diversity of our movement.

"The Feminist Movement has come a long way from its roots in the 19th century. ... But the fight for equal rights is not over."

We Still Need Feminism

Tamanna Mishra

In the following viewpoint, Tamanna Mishra argues that equality between the sexes is still a distant dream. The author then discusses several documentaries about the lives of women. Topics include the history of the women's rights movement and current aspects of legal rights. They cover stories from the United States and countries around the world. Topics include rape, sex slavery, the portrayal of women in the media, and the killing of baby girls. These documentaries show the challenges women face in the United States and the even greater challenges they face in some other countries. Tamanna Mishra is a writer and communications consultant. She primarily works in South and Southeast Asia and India.

"These Documentaries Will Tell You Why We Still Need Feminism in 2018," by Tamanna Mishra, YourStory Media Pvt. Ltd., March 7, 2018. Reprinted by permission. This article was originally published on your story(https://yourstory.com).

As you read, consider the following questions:

1. How can documentaries show the state of gender inequality, according to the viewpoint?
2. What are some challenges that women face across cultures, as mentioned in the documentaries?
3. Do the documentaries suggest that country, race, and class also play roles in equality?

The Feminist Movement has come a long way from its roots in the 19th century. Since then, women have gone on to work and vote, participate in the economy, and start businesses, and today appear to have far more agency over their lives and careers than ever before. But the fight for equal rights is not over. Sure, women go to work, but they get paid less for equal work. Women do get to vote, but getting to the top of the political hierarchy is still extremely difficult for them in most parts of the world, even in the US. They get catcalled on the roads, rape is on the rise, girls' parents are still paying dowry, and female infanticide is still a reality. There is still sexism everywhere—at work, in family meals, in colleges, on the streets. We are in 2018, and while a lot has changed, true equality is still a very, very long way off.

Fortunately, these stories of challenge and daily struggles have not gone unheard. We looked around for some of the best documentaries that speak of women's issues at length if we are willing to listen and understand. These documentaries span developed and developing economies and geographies from around the globe, and go on to show that our challenges might be different, but equality is equally important—and still a long way off—for women in most parts of the world.

She's Beautiful When She's Angry

Start at the very beginning and see what went into the making of the turning point of the women's rights movement. *She's Beautiful When She's Angry* is the inspiring story of the courageous, brilliant, and often outrageous women of the 1960s women's rights movement. The documentary takes us through the founding of the National Organization of Women to more radical factions of the movement such as the street battles of a group called Women's International Conspiracy From Hell, also known as WITCH. The documentary includes dramatizations, performances, and archived visuals, and tells the stories of women who started a global revolution while fighting for their own rights.

Equal Means Equal

Equal Means Equal takes a critical view of how women are treated in the western world 50 years after the women's rights movement. It delves into the legal aspects of equal rights. Director Kamala Lopez uses real-life stories and precedent-setting legal cases to showcase how outdated mindsets and laws influence cases of domestic violence, rape, sexual assualt, workplace harassment, and wage gap, among other issues plaguing women. The film strongly advocates for law amendments in favour of women and showcases the urgent need for them using strong real-life examples.

Finding Home

The documentary chronicles the personal stories of three Cambodian women who were forced into sex trafficking due to economic challenges. Beyond the story of how they got into the business, *Finding Home* showcases the challenges and struggles of being low-rung in the power hierarchy of slave owners and exploitative men. The Cambodian women heal over the years and put their lives back together after years of struggling with the unique challenges that are part of this exploitative trade. They live to tell the tale, and Finding Home does an empathetic job of it.

The Hunting Ground

What could be a safer space for women than schools and colleges, right? *The Hunting Ground* proves you wrong as it chronicles the horrifying stories of rape, sexual assault, and harrassment of girls in college campuses. The documentary takes a view of the staggering statistics of rape culture in academic institutes—one in five women in US college campuses are sexually assaulted—and why only a small fraction of these cases are reported, and even fewer result in justice for the victims. It sheds light on the systemic cover-up, rationalization, victim-blaming, and denial at the peripheries of the real issue—women are not safe even in their own colleges.

Miss Representation

Media—films, TV, advertising—had the potential to showcase women in influential positions and create role models. But they wasted this opportunity in favour of attracting male viewers and encouraged outdated views of gender roles by making women either plot objects or self-sacrificing housewives. In 2018, we can still count on our fingers the number of TV shows, movies, and ads around the world that showcase women as realistic or influential. Even when they try, they often get it all wrong. *Miss Representation* takes a critical view of this missed opportunity. It interweaves real-life stories of teenage girls with interviews with powerful feminists from politics and media, including Hillary Clinton, Ellen Degeneres, Dolly Parton, Oprah Winfrey, and Sarah Palin, among others. The underlying message in the documentary is the urgent need for role model portrayals in the media, or as the documentary says, "If you can't see it, you can't be it."

It's a Girl: The Three Deadliest Words in the World

It is 2018 and women have more rights and agency than ever before. Yet, in India, China, and several other parts of the world, unborn girls are aborted and newborn girls are killed or abandoned, because they are girls. Young girls who survive this first attack on their lives often grow up with less nutrition compared to their male counterparts, even in their own homes. They eat at the end of family meals after the best parts of the food are consumed by the men of the family—and this is if they are lucky. If they are not, they go on to face extreme domestic violence and dowry deaths.

The statistics of gender-based violence in many parts of the world, not in the least in India, are staggering.

The power equations and cultural dynamics causing gender disparity have not changed in many circles, even the seemingly elite and educated ones. That is the story and the underlying message of *It's a Girl: The Three Deadliest Words in the World*. The documentary is shot in India and China and dives deep into the reasons behind this striking gender disparity that actually eliminates women from many circles of life. It pointedly asks why not enough has been done to save girls and women. Horrifying real-life stories of abandoned and trafficked girls, women who face dowry-violence, mothers who have fought to save their daughters, and mothers who would literally kill for a son make up this documentary. Solutions include interviews with experts and activists who have devoted their lives to advocate for social change through empowerment, education, and several other paths out of this injustice doled out to women and girls every single day of their lives.

Hooligan Sparrow

In this hard-hitting documentary about rape culture in China, film-maker Nanfu Wang and activist Ye Haiyan travel to the Hainan province to protest against the rape of six elementary school girls by their school principal. In the process, the activists get labelled as enemies of the state and face government surveilance, harassment, and even interrogation. *Hooligan Sparrow* was shot despite this hostility and intimidation. It uses secret recording devices and hidden cameras to expose the reality of rape culture in China. The film was released for public viewing only after the footage was smuggled out of the country. It chronicles the brave battle of Ye Haiyan and her fellow activists and their uphill battle against all odds for a very basic human right—the right for young girls to be safe in school.

India's Daughter

Speaking of rape culture, *India's Daughter* chronicles the situation closer home. In the aftermath of the 2012 rape and murder of Jyoti Singh, filmmaker Leslee Udwin and the BBC interviewed the victim's parents and one of the four men convicted of the rape and murder, Mukesh, along with his defendant AP Singh. What follows is a horrifying story of victim blaming, not only by society at large but also the unapologetic rapist and his defendant as well. Despite being banned by the Indian Government in 2015, the film was made available on the Internet and went viral because it resonated with everyone demanding an immediate change in social values that encourage such gory violence against women.

!Women Art Revolution

Art has long been not just a medium of expression for the oppressed but also a harbinger of change through awareness and expression. *!Women Art Revolution* chronicles the role of art in the women's rights movement. It showcases the rise of women's art communities around the world, starting from the feminist movement of '60s and '70s America. It includes archive visuals, interviews, and stories of activists like the Guerilla Girls, Yoko Ono, and Judy Chicago. Beyond women artistes, !Women Art Revolution also tells the story of gender politics in art communities.

Girl Rising

Focusing on education as a means to empowerment, *Girl Rising* is a documentary about nine girls from different parts of the world and their journey to basic education. The girls hail from Haiti, Nepal, Ethiopia, India, Egypt, Peru, Cambodia, Sierra Leone, and Afghanistan, and have braved horrifying injustices such as child marriage and slavery as well as circumstantial ones like geographic isolation and poor facilities. Girl Rising is the touching story of these girls and how they found their voices. It showcases the powerful and inspiring spirit of these girls, and at the same time, relentlessly advocates for the right to education as a powerful tool to empower girls around the world.

Half the Sky: Turning Oppression into Opportunity for Women Worldwide

The documentary is based on a 2009 nonfiction book of the same name by Nicholas Kristof and Sheryl WuDunn. *Half the Sky* travels to 10 countries around the world, including Afghanistan, Cambodia, Kenya, India, Liberia, Pakistan, Sierra Leone, Somalia, and Vietnam, to chronicle stories of gender-based oppression like trafficking, violence, rape, maternal mortality, and education. It also tells the stories of inspiring women who have risen against the odds and discusses meaningful and lasting solutions through better healthcare, right to education, and economic empowerment.

Sisters in Law

State prosecutor Vera Ngassa and Court President Beatrice Ntuba chronicle the plight of women in the West African country of Cameroon. Through four court cases of violence against women, *Sisters in Law* showcases the stories of these women seeking justice and change in favour of the rights and privileges of women and children living under Sharia Law in the country.

Blood on My Hands

In 2018, menstruation is still a taboo topic in many parts of Indian society and excludes women from religion, society, and households due to something as commonplace and biological as their menstruation cycles. *Blood on My Hands* sensitively relates the issues of puberty and sexuality of women in India. It interweaves the stories and opinions of men and women to showcase the weight this monthly phenomenon can have on the lives of women in India.

The Holy Wives

The Holy Wives is the story of the lives of Devdasi women in Andhra Pradesh and Karnataka who are raped in the name of tradition, some even as a minor. It dives deep into the struggles and psychology of these Devdasis, also known as Jogins, Basavis, Kalawants, Paravatis, or Mathammas, as they fight to maintain their self-respect and earn livelihoods in the aftermath of the Devdasi system getting banned in the two states. The ban did not bring any credible alternatives and has eventually led to the increase in trafficking of children and women, just to earn two square meals a day. *The Holy Wives* also touches upon the struggles of three other communities that have suffered at the hands of caste-based violence against women.

Izzatnagari ki Asabhya Betiyan

Izzatnagari ki Asabhya Betiyan chronicles the resistance against "honour killings" by Khap Panchayats in India. It tells the story of five young women from the Jat community who dared to take on the powerful Khap Panchayats in Haryana. In the process, these women confront murder, injustice, and the social boycott of women who make "mistakes" like getting married in the same gotra, getting married outside their castes, or sometimes, just having a say in the matter of their own marriage. The narratives of honour killing survivors are intertwined with interviews with the Khap. In the process, *Izzatnagari ki Asabhya Betiyan* exposes the inherent hypocrisy and violence against women in a country that promises equality for all through its democratic set up.

Honor Diaries

Honor Diaries is the story of nine brave women's rights advocates who are part of the gender equality discourse in the Middle East. The documentary also exposes the problem of political correctness that stops this extreme inequality from getting identified and addressed on a global scale. *Honor Diaries* delves deep into the psyche of a Middle East that has failed to provide basic rights to its women, such as freedom of movement, right to education, agency and choice in matters of marriage, and any opposition to institutionalised abuse like female genital mutilation. It is an attempt to move from storytelling to initiate a movement of sorts. *Honor Diaries* creates awareness about the issues of women in Muslim-majority societies and seeks the international solidarity needed for the lives of these women to change for the better.

Dark Girls

The 2012 documentary *Dark Girls* is about the stories of struggles and loneliness faced by dark-skinned girls around the world. It delves into the depths of classism and racism that has caused the ostracization of dark girls not just in the arranged marriage circles in India but around the world. An anthology of personal stories that expose the cultural beliefs and attitudes of societies against dark-skinned girls, *Dark Girls* also presents an opportunity for young girls to heal and accept themselves as they are against all odds and everything society might believe or say about them.

These documentaries do a brilliant job of moving from the superficialities of women's liberation to showcase the unique ways in which women continue to be ostracised—at home and work, in school, and in social setups. It is about time too—change can't come fast enough. Awareness is the first step towards real, unconditional gender equality. This Women's Day is as good a time as any to spread this awareness and spark new conversations in favour of a change in our workplaces and in our living rooms. How are you planning to go about it?

Periodical and Internet Sources Bibliography

The following articles have been selected to supplement the diverse views presented in this chapter.

Assaf, Jessica, "The Future is Feminine," Mar 15, 2018. https://medium.com/@jessicaassaf/the-future-is-feminine-3e13f1bf639b

Badham, Van, "That's patriarchy: how female sexual liberation led to male sexual entitlement," Guardian News and Media Limited, Feb 2, 2018. https://www.theguardian.com/commentisfree/2018/feb/02/thats-patriarchy-how-female-sexual-liberation-led-to-male-sexual-entitlement

Bendix, Trish, "What 'The Future Is Female' Really Means," Viacom International Inc., Oct 19, 2017. http://www.newnownext.com/tegan-and-sara-wildfang-the-future-is-fluid/10/2017/

"The Dangerous Feminine," Curators of the University of Missouri. https://maa.missouri.edu/gallery/dangerous-feminine

"Do we still need feminism?" Debating Europe. Apr 7, 2018. https://www.debatingeurope.eu/2018/07/04/do-we-still-need-feminism/#.XEi6DlxKjcs

Grigson, Natalie, "The Future is Female, but (I hope) Not Feminine," Waylon H. Lewis Enterprises, Aug 15, 2017. https://www.elephantjournal.com/2017/08/the-future-is-female-but-i-hope-not-feminine/

Invisible Atheist, "Why Modern Feminism Is a Bad Thing," May 2, 2015. https://invisibleatheist.wordpress.com/2015/05/02/why-modern-feminism-is-a-bad-thing-2/

Okolosie, Lola, "Is patriarchy really dead?" Guardian News and Media Limited, 17 Sep 2019. https://www.theguardian.com/commentisfree/2013/sep/17/patriarchy-hanna-rosin

Pufahl, Shannon, "The Future Is Feminine?" Stanford University. https://exploreintrosems.stanford.edu/sophomore/future-feminine

Tanner, Emma, "Women have the same opportunities as men in the workforce—they choose not to take them," University of Utah Student Media, Mar 9, 2015. http://dailyutahchronicle.com/2015/03/09/women-have-the-same-opportunities-as-men-in-the-workforce-they-choose-not-to-take-them/

VERVE Team, "Feminist Statistics: Why We Still Need Feminism." Jun 25, 2018. https://medium.com/verve-up/feminist-statistics-why-we-still-need-feminism-2ae62d277baf

Walker, Carlie, "Yes, we still need feminism—and this is why," Maryborough Hervey Bay Newspaper Company Pty Ltd, https://www.frasercoastchronicle.com.au/news/opinion-yes-we-still-need-feminism-and-why/3356841/

Weiss, Suzannah, "9 Things People Get Wrong About Being Nonbinary," *Teen Vogue*, Feb 15, 2018. https://www.teenvogue.com/story/9-things-people-get-wrong-about-being-nonbinary

Weiss, Suzannah, "7 Ways Women Are Expected To Perform Femininity On A Daily Basis," Jan 10 2017. https://www.bustle.com/p/7-ways-women-are-expected-to-perform-femininity-on-a-daily-basis-29171

OPPOSING
VIEWPOINTS®
SERIES

CHAPTER 3

What Is the Future of Masculinity?

Chapter Preface

In scientific terms, a male human has an X and a Y chromosome pair. Male animals may fertilize eggs, but they do not produce eggs or give birth to babies. If someone is masculine, they have the appearance or qualities traditionally associated with men. Often these qualities include strength and aggressiveness.

Men may be seen as warriors, protectors, and providers. These roles may be embraced and admired. And yet, in modern society, many people are quick to attack masculinity. It is often seen as dangerous and harmful. Most violence is committed by men. Most murderers, and nearly all mass murderers, are men. This leads some to wish masculinity could be eliminated. Is this realistic? Would it truly benefit society?

No matter how much harm masculinity can do, many people see it as valuable and even necessary. They may argue that masculine men do necessary work, including physically demanding and dangerous jobs. They may point out that many women are more attracted to masculine men.

Yet others argue that the patriarchy, which supports traditional masculinity, harms men as well as women. These critics may long for greater empathy, a quality more often associated with women. They may see feminism as a benefit to men, because feminism attempts to dismantle the patriarchy.

Is masculinity necessary for the survival of society, or is it a danger that could destroy our planet? Should people embrace masculinity or reject it in favor of feminism? Should they try to eliminate traditional masculinity and femininity or embrace a changing spectrum between the two? The viewpoint authors in this chapter present different dreams for the future of men and masculinity.

| "*I sense … confusion about what it means to be a good man in a world of wars, sex trade, economic stress, and mass murders.*"

Boys Want to Know How to Be Good Men

Tom Matlack

The following viewpoint was published shortly after a mass shooting at the Sandy Hook Elementary School in Newtown, Connecticut. A twenty-year-old male entered the school and shot and killed twenty children and six adult staff members. The viewpoint author, Tom Matlack, uses that tragic episode to introduce questions about masculinity. He discusses empathy, which is the ability to understand and share the feelings of other people. Tom Matlack is an author and entrepreneur. He founded the Good Men Project, which provides space for conversations about manhood. In his work with the organization, he speaks to many groups. He has found that boys and young men hunger for answers about what it means to be a good man.

"Why Our Boys Need the Good Men Project," by Tom Matlack, GoodMenProject.com, December 18, 2012. Reprinted by permission.

As you read, consider the following questions:

1. Why does one of the sources quoted recommend empathy for angry young white men?

2. What is the benefit in loving and empathizing with boys and men, according to the author?

3. Are boys and young men interested in how to be good men, according to the author?

In the wake of the mass slaughter of innocent children, the inevitable news cycle has moved on from the event itself to the question of why? What possibly could lurk in the heart of a young man to commit such atrocities? Access to guns? Mental illness? His very budding manhood? What is wrong with us as a country that we could allow such a horror to happen on our own shores while looking for the bad guys thousands of miles away the supposedly "primitive" nations of the Middle East?

I have no answers. I have limited my exposure to the news for myself and put a complete black out in place for my seven year-old. He doesn't know what happened. And I can only absorb the terror in bits and pieces.

One piece did catch my attention, however. A female French professor wrote in the *New York Times* about how this pattern of butchery is the dark underbelly of Hana Rosin's "End of Men." She didn't put it quite that way, but that's my interpretation. If you close your eyes and think of a mass murderer in your mind's eye, what kind of person do you imagine? The archetype is a young white man, according to Christy Wampole in *Guns and the Decline of the Young Man*:

> This image can only be attributed to the truth of those patterns that have established themselves, from Charles Whitman's 1966 shooting spree at the University of Texas, to Timothy McVeigh's 1995 Oklahoma City bombing, to the 1999 Columbine massacre, to Wade Michael Page's 2012 attack on the Sikh temple in Wisconsin. The mass murderer is a type. And his race is white.

Wampole goes on to say that the angry black man has been usurped by the angry white man. That many men feel the undercurrent of their loss of power, a la Rosen's data about women's gain in the workplace and higher education, and they are trying to hold it together on the outside. But inside they are boiling over. "All this, and they still are not allowed to cry," she says.

Her answer is empathy. Empathy for the angry young white man:

> Empathy is difficult because it forces us to feel the suffering of others. It is destabilizing to imagine that if we are lucky or blessed, it just as easily could have gone some other way. For the young men, whose position is in some ways more difficult than that of their fathers and grandfathers, life seems at times to have stacked the cards against them. It is for everyone to realize the capricious nature of history, which never bets consistently on one group over another. We should learn to cast ourselves simultaneously in the role of winner and loser, aggressor and victim.

I hate to admit that I stumbled across this article on Twitter where cyber feminists and Men's Rights advocates were having a field day with the theoretical implications of Ms. Wampole's piece. For those who believe in the blinding power of privilege, the concept that race and gender could have been flipped on its head in this country is abhorrent indeed. "To say that young white men need to be coddled through their transition out of power is infantilizing horse hockey. #rebootmasculinity" was the actual tweet that caught my attention and led me to the article.

Mass murders have been almost all white. And they have been young men who are profoundly disturbed.

My personal confidence in gender and racial theories that lead to grand conclusions as to the cause of these events is very low. I have no particular insight into the souls of the men who committed these acts of violence. And I am not about to start speculating.

But I do have a 16 year-old son and I have spent that last four years talking about manhood, so I have a few impressions that bear on the issue.

I've given well over a hundred talks on manhood by now, all across the country to a variety of different groups. For quite some time my standard line was that my best audiences were: women (who love to talk about men); inmates (they couldn't leave); and boys. That has actually changed. Last year I spoke at the Boston Book Festival to a crowd of 800 that was more than half guys dying to talk about manhood. But the thirst among boys has from the beginning been striking. And it continues to this day.

"The last time you could have heard a pin drop like that was a talk I had to give on oral sex," the headmaster of Belmont Hill School told me after I addressed his entire student body of the all male high school. The response was identical at the Epiphany School, an inner city school in the worse neighborhood of Boston where the headmaster installed radar on the roof to defer would be shooters. At Epiphany the African-American students, several of whom had to live in a local hospital until their foster arrangements were finalized, clung to the pages of our book—the spine broken down from multiple readings and pages dog-eared for our class discussion.

My observation, based only on what I have seen with my own eyes, is that race and economic status have little to do with the thirst for answers about manhood among teenaged boys. When Andre Tippet (yes it does help to bring along an NFL Hall of Famer when you want to get boys to sit up and take notice) talked about Karate as a form of discipline far more important than football, the boys soaked it up as some response to porn and MMO games. When I spoke of alcoholism and how my professional successes proved to be no comfort when I realized that I had failed as a father and husband early in my life, it was as if I had direct access to the hearts of boys who wanted to be good men, if only they could figure out what that meant.

At Epiphany we brought Julio Medina with us, a man who was once the head of the biggest drug gang in the South Bronx before getting busted by the Federal Task Force on Drugs and spending a decade inside Sing Sing. He talked about how in prison you never want to get blood on your uniform after a stabbing because you will either squeal and be stabbed yourself or refuse to talk and end up in solitary. And yet when his friend went down he didn't step over him as he had so many times before. He picked him up and held him close while he bled out. "I realized that this couldn't go on," he told them. And at that moment his life changed.

Even though I had heard Julio dozens of times before, when he told his story in Epiphany I could hear my own heart pounding. The young men in that room knew exactly the choice that Julio had made in that prison hallway. Their very presence at Epiphany meant that they had already chosen to smear themselves with the blood of goodness, despite all odds. But hearing Julio confirmed what the heroism of their actions.

My own son is a high school junior at a Jesuit school whose motto is, "Become a man for others." He has taken that ideal to heart, traveling to Haiti and the Dominican Republic to care for orphans, witness families living on huge trash dumps, and planting coffee in the mountains. He aspires to go to West Point not to kill but to serve. And I believe him.

I don't hold up my son as any kind of superman. I sense in him the same fear that I saw in the boys at Belmont Hill, at Epiphany, and every other school I have visited. The confusion about what it means to be a good man in a world of wars, sex trade, economic stress, and mass murders.

I always talk about how important it is to me to be a good father and husband when I talk to boys. I see manhood for my generation, but also the next, in this transition between bread-winner to home-warmer. The Stay-At-Home Dad is the hero in my mind, just like the Stay-At-Home Mom was and still is the unseen force for good. In the end to be good is to learn how to love, in my view. Or at least that's what's worked in my life.

Sometimes the scale of change and the assault of popular culture blinds our boys to the basic truths of humanity. Do we need to have empathy for our boys, specially the white ones? I suppose, though I am not so sure that white boys deserve any empathy above and beyond those boys of color I met at Epiphany.

I think all our boys need a forum like The Good Men Project to make them realize they are not alone, they are not hated, that what they see online in terms of sex and violence and manhood is a pale shadow of real manhood. We need to love our boys so they learn the power of their own love as husbands, fathers and men.

> "[M]en have an innate drive for aggression. ... That drive can be channeled toward building themselves and protecting those around them. Or it can be unleashed in waves of destruction. Or, alternatively, it can be tamped down, killed. Men can be emasculated."

Emasculation Is Not a Solution to Social Ills

Ben Shapiro

In the following viewpoint Ben Shapiro argues that there is a movement on the part of the political left to emasculate men. As a foundation for his argument, the author uses a tweet from entertainer Bette Midler. Shapiro uses the tweet as a launching pad to argue that men are innately aggressive and that disparaging and trying to tamp down their naturally "masculine" traits can lead to larger problems. Instead, he writes, these traits should be carefully cultivated, and young men should be taught how to be gentlemen rather than being "emasculated." Ben Shapiro is a conservative political commentator who writes columns for Newsweek *and* Creators Syndicate. *He is founder and editor in chief of the* Daily Wire.

"The 'Toxic Masculinity' Smear," by Ben Shapiro, National Review, June 7, 2017. Reprinted by permission.

As you read, consider the following questions:

1. Why did the author feel the urge to investigate a training program for men?
2. Is it rational for the author to base an entire argument on one celebrity's tweet?
3. What is "the truth" according to the author?

On Monday, the *New York Post* ran a story about Warrior Week, a boot camp for men run by Garrett J. White, "a 40-year-old blond with tattooed biceps who looked like a video-game soldier." For the low, low cost of just $25,000, White will run you through a regimen of physical torture and mental preparation that involves being punched in the face, hiking while holding logs, and reciting the poem "Invictus." White explained:

> We teach them how to be a man. … Women are leading across the board in business and at home . . . and living more powerfully than men today. And that's causing complete chaos for men.

The first question on the application for White's training program: "Have you ever been punched in the face by another man?"

Now, I have never been punched in the face. At least not as an adult, that is. When I was younger, I was routinely bullied—I was about 5 foot 2 throughout most of high school, since I was two years younger than the other students. That meant severe physical abuse and some relatively egregious torment at the hands of classmates.

Now I'm married, with two children of my own. I own several guns. I spend my days writing and speaking and thinking; I believe the fundamental proposition that Western civilization was built in order to prevent people from punching each other in the face.

But I'll admit that for a split second, I felt the urge to check out White's website. Why? Because men have an innate drive for aggression. They feel the need to test themselves against their limits. That drive can be channeled toward building themselves and protecting those around them. Or it can be unleashed in waves of destruction. Or, alternatively, it can be tamped down, killed. Men can be emasculated.

I thought about White when I read Bette Midler's tweet regarding the London terror attack last Saturday evening. Here's what the star of *Beaches* had to tell us: "More sorrow and grief at the hands of madmen in London. Men and religion are worthless."

Put aside the inanity of lumping together all religion as "worthless" thanks to the acts of radical Islamists, who are devotees of a religion she refuses to mention, presumably out of sheer cowardice. Focus instead on her belief that "men … are worthless." It's indicative of a general belief among members of the Left that masculinity itself is toxic and must be quashed. Hillary Clinton spoke last month at a Planned Parenthood gala where drinks called "toxic masculinity" were served; she explained that men are "doing everything they can to roll back the rights and progress we've fought so hard for over the last century." Men, you see, are the problem. Men make war; men commit crimes; men rape; men infuse their aggression into everything.

Midler and those of like mind are wrong to lump all men together, of course. It was male police officers who arrived to kill the terrorists. It is male soldiers attempting to liberate women from the depravity of ISIS terrorists. Males destroy, but males also build.

But in their effort to eradicate the destructive male tendency, the Left has pushed emasculation as a solution. While they champion the notion that women can do anything they set their minds to (true!), they simultaneously castigate men as the barriers to progress and masculinity as a condition to be avoided. The goal of the Left, therefore, becomes to train boys not to become men. Instead, boys should be feminized; they should never be encouraged to "be a man." That's too pressure-filled, too nasty, too mean.

But boys want to become men; men want to be men. As Christina Hoff Sommers points out: "Most boys evince healthy masculinity. … telling a boy to 'man up' can be harsh and degrading. But teaching him to 'be a gentleman' is another matter."

EQUALITY GOES AGAINST NATURE

The feminist movement has been and is, in effect, a rebellion against the laws of Nature and also against the very teachings and beliefs of historic Christianity. Whether it be the so-called modest reforms advocated in the 19th century—voting rights and property entailment and inheritance reform, or the more progressivist demands of the late twentieth century—military service equity, professional and job parity, unisex bathrooms, or the most recent insistence on same sex marriage, transgenderism, and gender fluidity, the movement is rubricked under the principle of "equality," that is, its proclaimed objective is the overturning of "restraints" on women and the complete equality of the sexes.

Yet, in fact, equality as envisaged by the feminists does not exist and has never existed in nature.

For feminism "equality" is a slogan, in reality an exercise in subterfuge employed to shame weak-willed (and weak-brained) men and to eventually dissolve the traditional social bonds and inherited natural (and moral) laws that have governed our culture for two millennia.

If men are not told to be "gentlemen," some will be emasculated, but more will become destructive men. If men are not trained by good men, they will be trained by bad men; if they have no good males to follow, they follow bad ones. The Left routinely speaks about a world run by women and why such a world would create better men. But the most male-free environment in America exists in black communities, where well over half of black children grow up without fathers. This hasn't made black boys less violent; it's made them far more prone to criminality than their non-black peers. Many of these boys follow teenage role models, many of whom have lacked fathers themselves, and lack the training to be a gentleman. They live in a world of risk that requires masculine

Whether from the Prophets of the Old Testament, or from the incredibly rich inheritance of ancient philosophy, or from St. Paul and the consistent teachings of the Church, there has been an understanding that there are discernible "laws" in nature, the orderly functioning of which made society and social arrangements possible, even harmonious. What the Christian church did, following on the acute observations of the Ancients, was to confirm both spiritually and doctrinally the existence and appositeness of those laws, for they were integral to creation, itself.

The destruction of masculinity and emasculation of men has been perhaps the most grievous and disastrous consequence of the "women's movement." For centuries—indeed, not that long ago—an inherited code of honor, deference and respect, how to treat women, prevailed in Western society. While, it is true, certain functions and roles were generally not open to women historically, that in no way dimmed or lessened their critical importance and paramount position in society. Indeed, as child bearers and mothers it was they most uniquely who governed the essential running of the family and palpably were the primary and substantial foundation of society.

"What Has Happened to Masculinity in the 21st Century?" by Boyd D. Cathey, Chronicles: A Magazine of American Culture, September 27, 2018.

defense but have no one to teach them to distinguish between defense and aggression.

The Left's dichotomous choice between emasculation and toxic masculinity leaves men out in the cold—and leaves them searching for meaning. If they are not the defenders of their families, what are they? If they are not providers, what are they? They become non-entities—or they become societal tumors or at least tacit supporters of "men who are men!"

It doesn't take being punched in the face to be a man. I'm not signing up for White's class. But that's because my father taught me to be a gentleman: to protect my family and my community, to stand up for good things, to build rather than destroy. And to train my own son the same way.

But in a society that denies manhood altogether, that denies men's special protective and creative role in society—or worse, categorizes masculinity as mere violence—it's easy to fall into a simplistic self-identification with toxic manhood. The age of emasculation cannot last. It will eventually boil over into violence, sink away into irrelevance, or return to the truth: that the male aggressive instinct can be good but must be trained, not excised.

> *"Speaking about the masculinity crisis detracts our attention from a real issue: our failure to reform the way we think about masculinity and how unfit it is for the culture in which we now live."*

There Is Not a "Masculinity Crisis"

Aneta Stępień

In the following viewpoint, Aneta Stępień argues that debates surrounding a supposed masculinity crisis do more harm than good. The author explains that boys are taught to be tough and suppress their feelings. Such avoidance can breed aggression and resentment. This can have disastrous results for individuals and society, such as abuse and violence against others and health problems, depression, and suicide among men. The author suggests that men should be encouraged to open up to emotions and vulnerability rather than to mourn the potential extinction of behavior that has been associated with masculinity. Aneta Stępień is adjunct assistant professor at Trinity College Dublin's School of Languages, Literatures and Cultural Studies.

As you read, consider the following questions:

1. What is the result of boys being taught to reject emotion and vulnerability?
2. What is a "masculinity crisis" according to the viewpoint?
3. How can language help or hurt the issue according to the author?

The recent outpouring of sexual harassment cases makes people wonder: what is wrong with men? After all, the vast majority of those accused of sexual violence are men. The simple and perhaps shocking answer is that we, as a society, tell men to be violent. We speak about "real" manhood and call men to "grow a pair" to prove they are manly enough.

And, crucially, we describe men's anxieties about their changing social roles as a "masculinity crisis."

In doing this, we suggest that manhood is something universal, even primeval, and thus unchangeable. But masculinity is a social construct. It has a history.

Our ideals of masculinity—the model to which men are supposed to aspire—is very old-fashioned. Even though our culture changed drastically over the course of the 20th century, the qualities we value in "real men"—such as domination, control, physical strength and emotional restraint—are unchanged. These qualities were promoted during the high period of European imperialism in the 19th century—when nations sought above all else to dominate other cultures.

As boys grow up, their peers, parents and even girlfriends tell them "boys don't cry," "don't be a girl," "be strong." They learn to feel ashamed of emotionality and vulnerability. They are expected to "prove" their masculinity and, often, that means aggression. Sociologists and psychologists, such as Stephen M. Whitehead, or Victor J. Sadler tell us that only by connecting with their emotions can men look at themselves critically and change their behaviour.

Another old belief is that men can become "real men" through sexual conquest. In 1886, Richard von Krafft-Ebing wrote in Psychopathia Sexualis, the most influential book on human sexuality, that for men, sex with women was a biological force, a "natural instinct … demanding fulfilment." The idea that healthy men need to satisfy their instinct through sex was commonly accepted as the truth—the norm regulating relations between men and women. So the traditional and still dominant idea of masculinity means accepting and even encouraging male sexual conquest, the man's power over others and emotional restraint.

However, emotions, including sympathy and empathy, are actually crucial for healthy social interactions. Thanks to them we understand how other people feel and know how to respond properly—including responses to sexual harassment.

Changing Roles

More recently, we've begun to talk about a "masculinity crisis"—commonly used to describe how the changing work patterns and new family demands put pressure on men who feel distress and insecurity about their new gender role. Many straight men find it hard to reconcile the traditional view of gender with the new approach based on partnership and equality of men and women at home and in work. The sense of failing to perform the male ideal promoted by advertisement, Hollywood films and porn movies can provoke defensive reactions in men—machismo, resentment towards women and all-too often aggressive or abusive behaviour.

Clearly, the problem doesn't lie simply in the pressures of the changing culture but in the old-fashioned ideals of masculinity that can often only be achieved through predatory and sexist attitudes towards women. Sexism is a huge part of bonding among men who define themselves as heterosexual. Let's be clear, the sort of thing that Donald Trump refers to as "locker room talk" is not just banter, it's an accepted, encouraged and repeated practice of objectifying and denigrating women. Many men also find it difficult to speak out if they object to it.

A man who is sexist can't be a woman's ally—so why do we continue to value masculinity based on sexism? Even though this outdated and restrictive model of masculinity actually makes men unhappy, it prevails because the culture at large continues to enable it.

Redefining Masculinity

Speaking about the masculinity crisis detracts our attention from a real issue: our failure to reform the way we think about masculinity and how unfit it is for the culture in which we now live. The crisis narrative can become an easy excuse of inaction, or a handy justification of some men's violent and abusive behaviour.

The word "crisis" even seems to fuel a backlash against movements such as #metoo. When some men feel their status is under threat, blogs such as The Voice for Men emerge producing sexist content blaming women for the challenges faced by men.

While it's extremely important to discuss the changing roles and position of men, the language we use to do that has crucial consequences. The Irish campaign "Man up" is one example how to teach, particularly young boys, positive values and change the meaning we understand strength in men. This project promotes men's strength as not being in muscles but in active participation of men in preventing domestic violence.

The campaign also encourages men to speak up about their emotions because "silence can kill." The high number of suicide among men before their 50s is linked to men's restraint in sharing their emotions.

The negative narrative of the crisis stops men from joining the debate that there can be multiply ways of being a man and there is no shame in breaking with the old patterns.

Turning the story into something more positive—inviting men to actively participate in redefining the norms of masculinity—is how our concept of masculinity can be reformed. We should ditch the word "crisis" when speaking about the experiences of boys and men to end the cycle of recrimination.

> "*Patriarchy invites men to make a deal with the devil: trade your eternal wholeness and humanity, in exchange for earthly and temporal power.*"

Embrace a New Masculinity

Aaron Rose

In the following viewpoint Aaron Rose explores the idea of divine or healthy masculinity. The author says that the goal is not to erase gender differences. Rather, people should reclaim the original gender archetypes that flow within everyone. They can also embrace a wider spectrum of gender identity and expression. He suggests specific exercises people can do to explore and challenge their ideas about masculinity. Then they can choose what masculinity means to them and embrace that. Aaron Rose is a transman, a freelance journalist, and a diversity activist. The Numinous is a platform that promotes valuing feelings alongside facts.

"What is the Future of Masculinity?" by Aaron Rose, The Numinous. This article originally appeared on, and is being reprinted with the permission of, The-Numinous.com.

As you read, consider the following questions:

1. What is true masculinity, according to the viewpoint author?
2. Why should people challenge their beliefs about men and masculinity, according to the author?
3. What is the future of masculinity, according to this viewpoint?

W hen Now Age mystics speak of "divine masculinity," what they are describing is simply: masculinity. Exalted qualities of heart-centered action, fierce loyalty, innovative logic, and earthly strength are what masculinity truly is. Everything else is an aberration, a mistaken idea, and a misuse of energy.

The divine masculine is complemented by the divine feminine archetype: the universal energy of intuition, receptivity, nurturance, creation, and collaboration. These energies are not inherently gendered. They flow within all of us.

So how do we reclaim healthy or conscious masculinity? How do we end our crisis of sexual violence? How do we build a world with true gender equality?

In the #metoo era, it can sometimes feel like the goal is total eradication of an inherently "toxic masculinity," an embrace of androgyny, or an exclusive exaltation of the feminine. But the destination of our evolution is not about erasing our differences or course correcting from toxicity to divinity; it's about reclaiming gendered archetypes while embracing an even wider spectrum of expression.

Patriarchy is the collectively held (and externally manifested) idea that men are superior to people of other genders, that there are right and wrong ways to be men and women, and that there are rewards for reinforcing these ideas, and penalties for violating them.

And if patriarchy is a result and a manifestation of parasitic scarcity consciousness, then we're more than ready for abundant symbiosis.

A Different Way to Be Human

When I first began my transition from female to male, I was terrified of becoming a man. It was who I was—a person who had been female-assigned at birth and who felt called to a male identity and masculine embodiment—and yet, I could not have been more scared.

As a woman, I had lived a life defined and constrained by male violence—from the abuse of family members, to the harassment of strangers on the subway, and the subtle discrimination at work. The manhood I saw around me did not represent the kind of person I wanted to be. And the people I loved were quick to reinforce this idea: You'll become a tool of the patriarchy, they said. The world doesn't need another MAN.

On a physiological level, I knew that taking testosterone (in the form of hormone replacement therapy) was right for me. My body needed it, hungered for it like a too-late dinner after a long day. But on an emotional level, I was paralyzed, wracked by immobilizing guilt.

I was afraid of losing the part of myself that cries at Pixar movies and gathers my friends into huge hugs and composes love letters to my beloveds. The part who really, really listens to my people when they're hurting. I was afraid of embodying toxic masculinity. I was afraid of becoming (even more of) a stranger to myself.

This deterministic model of gender is one we're all used to. We've all heard "that's just how men are" and any number of absolutist statements that divide the population squarely down the middle, into two prescribed boxes: man and woman. I was just as trapped as anyone.

But equally, in making the choice to transition I knew I was signing up for a lifetime commitment to proving the idea that there was another way to be a man than what I had been shown. That ultimately, there was a different way to be a human altogether.

Revolutionizing Masculine Values

Tim Patten has released his sixth book on January 4, 2018. "Masculinity Is Our Future" is an unapologetic and realistic understanding of what being masculine means and how those who possess its modern traits are lionized, celebrated and valued.

"After the women's movement produced outstanding equity results for women and gays, it bankrupted its reputation by inventing false facts and institutionally disrespecting masculinity and natural male qualities," stated Patten. "Modern women's studies are indoctrinating young people into an untruthful caste system theory with one-sided facts such as patriarchy, declaring a male powered society is oppressive and not protective of women. This societal male-bashing has resulted in a mere 8 percent of support for feminism in the UK, it is killing the women's movement."

Millions have already joined the throngs of rebels, armchair enthusiasts and a growing swelling of the public are coming together in a counterculture movement that values, respects and nurtures masculine virtues. Patten said, "Men have been reviled, withstood invalidation, and called toxic for more than four decades. However, *Masculinity is Our Future* represents an insurgency, a massive underground awareness that is transgressive, inclusive and determined to change old-school gender narratives."

Patten contends the pendulum has swung too far, paying attention to only women's needs for the past four decades, ultimately ignoring men's health issues, leaving boys and men lagging behind girls and women across the entire educational system and suffering from a suicide epidemic.

"'Masculinity Is Our Future' Sets Out to Revolutionize Masculine Virtues," by Tim Patten, PR Newswire Association LLC., January 8, 2018.

Dismantling the Deal with the Devil

This commitment, this faith in the future of masculinity, has fueled my decade's plus of evolving work in diversity and inclusion—a key part of which is leading conscious masculinity workshops in which men and masculine people of all genders have an opportunity to take themselves off of cultural autopilot and reclaim healthy masculinity.

Patriarchy invites men to make a deal with the devil: trade your eternal wholeness and humanity, in exchange for earthly and temporal power.

Time and again, I witness men become emotional in my workshops when we talk about gender equality and allyship. When I ask why, they say things like: "I feel like I don't have anything else to offer," or "What more do you want from me?," or "Not everyone gets to be treated so nicely, you know."

As the conversations unfold, we identify, again and again, that they are fundamentally bewildered about why or how they should be giving something to someone else that they do not feel they have themselves: gentleness, a reason to truly accept themselves, a full range of self-expression, emotional presence.

In my workshops, we inventory our masculinity stories, going all the way back to our first memories. And themes emerge, like the first moment of shame, often attached to a memory of playing with feminine clothing, hugging other boys, or crying when we were sad. We bring loving witness to these wounds, and then we choose again.

If the story was: "when I am emotional, the people I love reject me"—we elect to write a new story: "my vulnerability brings me closer to the people I care about."

What Is Your Role in This Process?

Here are 4 ways we can all help bring about the future of masculinity:

1. Separate Masculinity and Femininity from Gender Identity and Sex Assigned at Birth

"Sex assigned at birth" is the label you were assigned at birth based on the external anatomy your doctor observed. Gender identity is your innate, internal, sense of your gender.

Within our current western gender model, which has its origins in European colonization and white supremacist social control, sex assigned at birth, gender, and gendered energy are all conflated. If you are male assigned at birth, it is assumed you will be a man, and that you will behave in a masculine way. This deterministic model belies the truth of our experience — the truth that indigenous people of many cultures have always embraced — that there are as many possible genders and gendered experiences as there are people.

For example, I currently have a pretty masculine embodiment—short hair, muscles, a deep voice, a flat chest, traditionally male clothing. However, my energy is a blend of masculine and feminine—I am a go-getter who is often charging forward on the next big idea AND I create space for the people I love to be vulnerable, where I too surrender into vulnerability with them.

We all contain both masculinity and femininity. The unique mix and balance of this energy within us is as essential as the flow of oxygen into our lungs and bloodstream.

2. Conduct a Patriarchal Thought Detox

What are the stories you're telling yourself about men and masculinity, and about gender overall? Do an inventory of your beliefs about masculinity and men, and choose some different stories.

Some of our big collective stories that you may have running on cruise control include: men should not be emotional, women are more emotional and nurturing than men, there are only two genders, men are just like that, what your body looks like determines your gender, and more.

Set a timer for 10 minutes, write these old stories out, and then decide what you want to replace them with. Write down your new narratives and reread them out loud every day for 21 days.

One my biggest autopilot scripts was that conscious men are few and far between, and that if I was really myself and spoke about gender the way I do, then I would have few connections with men, personally and professionally. I'm choosing to tell a different story now, to affirm that conscious stewards of masculine energy are all around me. And you know what? Bit by bit that community is emerging.

3. Understand That This Work Is Not Just for "Bad Guys"

When I discuss my conscious masculinity work, I often witness men immediately deciding that it's not for them. Or women deciding that it's not for their husband or their brother or their friend. Because they're already "good." They haven't assaulted anyone recently. They don't make gross jokes.

We have this mainstream idea that there are "those guys," those really bad guys, who have really messed up, who really need to get their act together. They're the problem. They're the patriarchy. They're the ones who need an intensive on conscious masculinity. But the truth is that this work is for ALL of us. We all have an opportunity and a responsibility to become stewards of a new era of masculinity, of gender, of humanity.

4. Embrace and Reclaim the Masculinity Within Yourself

No matter your gender, you contain an alchemical blend of both masculinity and femininity within yourself. How does your masculinity manifest? In the clothes you wear? In the role you play in your relationships? In the way you tackle a project or negotiate a deal? In the fictional characters you identify with and seek to emulate? How conscious is your masculinity? How much have you chosen it, rather than operating it on autopilot? What do you love about your masculinity? How does it symbiotically complement and amplify your femininity? What do you wish others could see about it?

Write a love letter to your masculinity. Honor what you learn about yourself in the process.

5. Practice Inviting Others into this Conversation

Where do you see others running on autopilot about masculinity and femininity? Maybe you're a mom and you see how other parents assume so much about their children based on their sex assigned at birth. Assuming how their child's body looks determines what their gender will be. Assuming boys will be tough and girls will like pink. Assuming girls will be nurturing and boys will be adventurous.

Just the other day I spoke with a mother who was grappling to understand why her 8-year-old son had been described by a teacher as "sensitive" and "safe" for the other kids to play with, because of how gentle and unaggressive he was. "I would have no problem seeing my daughter this way," she said. "But it's hard to compute how a boy could be described like that. It's not how I see him."

Maybe you're a man and you are aware of how conditioned you are to not call out other men when they say something sexist, or to shame each other for expressing emotion. Maybe you're a woman who feels super supported by your community of women, but feels like your male partner, family member, or friend, isn't conscious of his masculinity and how it impacts you.

It's okay to call the people into your life into greater accountability and connection. To do this, get honest about what your unique role is, however uncomfortable or scary it might feel. Whoever you are, your voice matters, and others will resonate with it.

A Manifesto for Conscious Masculinity

The work of remaking our relationship to masculinity and femininity is, like all other fundamentally spiritual work, ultimately about restoring our capacity to self-determine our identity, to trust our intuition, and to unconditionally love ourselves.

We are the generational clean-up crew, taking ourselves off of the autopilot our ancestors ran for centuries, mending the wounds they did not know how to tend. As we emerge from the shadow, it is our birthright to embody unprecedented levels of self expression, connection, and ease. It is the work of a lifetime, but it's why we're here. And we don't have to do it alone.

The future of masculinity is not an erasure of the traditional masculine archetype (ie strong, rugged, powerful, action-oriented), but a conscious release of the shadow sides of these traits (domination, control, emotional suppression, violence) and a conscious choosing of what our masculinity means to us.

The future of masculinity is the reclamation of this true divine masculine archetype, by whoever resonates most deeply with that energy.

The future of masculinity is amends and repair for generations of harm done, the honest reckoning of personal and collective shame and grief for violence committed, or violence not stopped.

The future of masculinity is an embrace of action without aggression, of leadership without dominance, of impetus and initiation without steamrolling, of grace without repression.

The future of masculinity is creation without collateral damage, strength without silencing, devotion without obsession, responsibility without control, power with rather then power over.

The future of masculinity is the intentional embrace of intuition, rather than the unconscious whim of instinct.

In short, it is a human life, fully and bravely lived, with self-love and connection with a Universal intelligence at its core, with nothing to prove and everything to share.

> "*Straight men owe a significant debt to gay men who have spent many years questioning masculinity and laying the groundwork for freedoms that all men now have the ability to enjoy.*"

Queer Masculinity Benefits Us All

Joseph Gelfer

In the following viewpoint, Joseph Gelfer examines gender fluidity. This is when gender expression shifts between masculine and feminine. Society tends to assume that anyone who doesn't follow traditional gender roles is gay. However, the author notes, people can be queer without being gay. Society will benefit if we can separate the concepts, he suggests. That would allow straight man to support dismantling traditional masculinity. In his view, greater gender fluidity will help all people—men, women, and nonbinary people, regardless of their sexual identity. Joseph Gelfer is a British author who covers masculinity and spiritual and religious topics.

"Queer Masculinity for Everyone," by Joseph Gelfer, GoodMenProject.com, September 18, 2016. Reprinted by permission.

As you read, consider the following questions:

1. How is "queer" different from "gay," according to the author?
2. What does the author mean by "queering gender"?
3. What is the advantage to straight men critiquing masculinity, according to the article?

You may have noticed the extraordinary rise in discussion lately referring to gender-fluidity, bisexuality, pansexuality and queerness of various stripes. This discussion rightly celebrates the diversity of sexual expression out there in the world, giving ever-greater voice to people who are not straight, and generally troubling the gay-straight binary that underpins most people's understanding of sexuality. But in celebrating this multiplicity of sexual orientations, these discussions fall into a trap that undermines a greater goal of evolving our perceptions around gender: namely, the faulty assumption that gender-fluidity is only about non-heterosexual orientations.

Queer is Not Necessarily Gay

While queerness was undoubtedly born out of the experiences of gay and lesbian people, being queer is not necessarily the same thing as being gay. In a theoretical sense, queerness is about challenging categorization. We can use queer as a verb: if something is queered, the parameters that define it are subverted or made strange.

When we unhook "queer" from "gay," certain things start to make sense that might otherwise appear confusing. If you're in the UK you might have seen the TV show about masculinity presented by Grayson Perry: a man who likes wearing women's clothes who has a wife. If you're in the US you might have seen the images of Young Thug, another man who likes to wear women's clothing but by most other markers is straight. These men are queer, but they are not gay.

To demonstrate this disconnect further, in the other direction, being gay does not necessarily make you queer. Numerous gay people adhere to standard gender roles, replicating stereotypical heterosexuality in various ways down to having children, living behind a white picket fence and adhering to traditional conservative political values: this is called "homonormativity."

But this distinction between "queer" and "gay" is rarely acknowledged, and this has two problematic effects. First, there is the assumption that anything to do with gender-bending is only about people who do not identify as straight. Second, people who "feel straight" sexually but "think queer" are nudged towards identifying with some form of non-straight sexual identity that may not be representative of their truth. Certainly, the gay-straight binary is forced upon us and there are probably many more people than we imagine who are neither one nor the other. But equally, in the spirit of freedom we must allow for people to be predominantly and unapologetically straight in terms of sexual orientation whilst being completely queer in how they perceive gender. Indeed, not only should this be allowed, it should be encouraged. If we have a goal of queering gender (in other words, subverting it, and breaking down harmful parameters), and this is only perceived as a "gay issue," the number of people we can reach is relatively small (even if we go with the high end of estimates for the number of people who do not identify as straight). In other words, reaching the tipping point of queering gender must involve straight people.

Queer Liberation for Straight Men

Once "queer" and "gay" are unhooked, queerness becomes a much easier sell to straight men. People need to realize that it is entirely possible for a straight-identifying man with a traditionally red-blooded attraction to women to be completely bent when it comes to how he perceives masculinity. There is no contradiction between finding women attractive and wanting to dismantle everything about traditional masculinity and replace it with something entirely different.

Indeed, the widespread realization of this fact could prove to be an extraordinary catalyst for getting men to challenge masculinity who are currently oppressed by our common understanding of what straightness means but who are nevertheless unable in good faith to embrace non-straightness as a way of connecting with their inner queer. It could well be that the word "queer" will never fully be unhooked from gayness and a different vocabulary is necessary to explain the same thing, such as Stage 4 on The Five Stages of Masculinity.

Further still, it may be that queerness is even more powerful coming from straight men than gay men. When a gay man critiques masculinity it is easily dismissed by straight men as they tend to think it is some kind of gay propaganda that has little to do with them. However, when a straight man critiques masculinity, other straight men cannot dismiss it so easily. Of course, it is important here not to erase gay men and their specific experiences and contributions to the discussion. Straight men owe a significant debt to gay men who have spent many years questioning masculinity and laying the groundwork for freedoms that all men now have the ability to enjoy.

Thinking Queer is More Important than Looking Queer

Much of the media reporting of queerness not only makes the mistake of assuming queerness is about sexual orientation, but that queerness requires people to look queer. Endless articles can be found that show gender-fluid types wearing clothing that is not obviously masculine or feminine, or who even parade some kind of gay carnival aesthetic. Even within the gay community, this has always resulted in gay people who look "normal" feeling somehow exiled and lacking. And in the current context, this results in queerness being reduced not just to gayness, but to a fashion statement. This season's fashions that are "changing masculinity" really have nothing to do with masculinity, rather the cut of cloth. Ultimately, it is far more important to think queer than to look queer. The widespread realization of this fact will also contribute to straight men having an easier time of embracing their inner queer.

In the end, the increasing acceptance of gender-fluidity is a positive and important step forward in our understanding of masculinity and our ability to rethink it in a way that results in a more sustainable future for all. But let's not pigeonhole gender-fluidity in such a way that it becomes inaccessible to the majority of people: we need queer masculinity for everyone, not just the few.

Periodical and Internet Sources Bibliography

The following articles have been selected to supplement the diverse views presented in this chapter.

Allen, Becky, "Hacking the Gender Gap: Why the Tech Industry Needs More Women," Council on Foreign Relations, Jul 20, 2016. https://www.cfr.org/blog/hacking-gender-gap-why-tech-industry-needs-more-women

"As gender roles change, are men out of step?" CBS News, Jun 17, 2012. https://www.cbsnews.com/news/as-gender-roles-change-are-men-out-of-step/

Cathey, Boyd D., "What has happened to masculinity in 21st century?" Chronicles: A Magazine of American Culture, Sep 27, 2018. https://www.chroniclesmagazine.org/what-has-happened-to-masculinity-in-21st-century/

"The Changing Role of the Modern Day Father," American Psychological Association. http://www.apa.org/pi/families/resources/changing-father.aspx

Clay, Rebecca A., "Redefining masculinity Three psychologists strive to build a 'better' man," American Psychological Association, Jun 2012. https://www.apa.org/monitor/2012/06/masculinity

Collazo, Abigail, "The Future of Masculinity: Do We Need Real Men - Or Real Human Beings?" Alternet, Jul 26, 2012. http://www.alternet.org/visions/future-masculinity-do-we-need-real-men-or-real-human-beings

Fradet, Philippe Leonard. "Beyond the 'Nice Guy': Creating a New Masculinity in the 21st Century," The Body is Not an Apology, Jan 5, 2017. https://thebodyisnotanapology.com/magazine/nice-guy-on-identifying-a-new-masculinity-part-1/

Monk, Carolyn, "How Patriarchy Hurts Men And Women," Feb 27, 2017, Odyssey. https://www.theodysseyonline.com/how-patriarchy-hurts-men-and-women

Morse, Brandon, "The Attack on Masculinity Is In Full Swing, But It Will Ultimately Fail", RedState.com, June 20, 2018. https://www.redstate.com/brandon_morse/2018/06/20/attack-masculinity-full-swing-will-ultimately-fail/

Myers, Jack, "What It Means to Be a 'Real Man' Today," Future of Men Movement, Apr 14, 2017. http://futureofmen.com/2017/04/what-it-means-to-be-a-real-man-today/

Sánchez, Erika L., "4 Ways Sexist, Macho Culture Hurts Men," Everyday Feminism, Sep 6, 2014. http://everydayfeminism. com/2014/09/macho-culture-hurts-men/

Segran, Elizabeth, "Rebranding The American Man," *Fast Company*, Mar 14, 2016. http://555.990.myftpupload.com/2017/03/ rebranding-the-american-man-fast-company/

Weiss, Bari, "Camille Paglia: A Feminist Defense of Masculine Virtues," *Wall Street Journal*, Dec. 28, 2013. https://www.wsj. com/articles/a-feminist-defense-of-masculine-virtuesa-feminist-defense-of-masculine-virtues-1388181961

Rich, John D. Jr. "Strict Gender Roles Hurt Men, Too," *Psychology Today*, Sussex Publishers, LLC, Mar 21, 2018. https://www. psychologytoday.com/us/blog/parenting-purpose/201803/strict-gender-roles-hurt-men-too-0

OPPOSING
VIEWPOINTS®
SERIES

CHAPTER 4

What Is the Future of Gender?

Chapter Preface

Gender roles are changing, as people debate what it means to be feminine or masculine. In the United States, women and men are converging in many areas. Women are more career minded than in previous generations, while men are more concerned about work-life balance. Younger people, in particular, are changing their views on gender and embracing greater equality between the sexes. However, in many countries, gender equality remains a distant dream. Many factors play into this issue. One is simply that many men don't want to give up their power. For people who are used to being on top, being equal feels like a loss.

Gender inequality can have severe, even deadly, effects. In countries where women are not valued, fewer girl babies are allowed to live. When women gain more opportunities in the workforce, they still often keep traditional responsibilities at home. They must work and take care of family members and the house. This means women may work much longer hours than men, some of those hours unpaid. On the other hand, men who lose power in the workforce often don't take on additional roles in the family. This can cause feelings of worthlessness. Rates of alcoholism, suicide, and depression may rise. This means gender equality is not only a human rights issue; it affects a country's population and economy.

A relatively new trend sees more people identifying as nonbinary: They do not identify with either gender. This can cause confusion and challenges in the workplace. Companies and government agencies may not allow people to identify themselves as nonbinary. And yet, some people claim that the future will be nonbinary. Will that help or harm gender equality? Will it allow straight men to deny their privileged position in society? Will it further demonize and suppress women? Or will it allow all people to flourish as their authentic selves, not bound to old-fashioned roles? The viewpoints in this chapter explore the way the world may change when it comes to gender.

> " 'Taken together, these two trends suggest that millennial women are on a similar footing with their male colleagues when it comes to career ambitions and expectation,' the report said."

Gender Roles Are Changing

Katherine Lewis

In the following viewpoint, Katherine Lewis discusses research into changing gender roles. She reports on a survey that is now several years old. The research discovered that young women are increasingly likely to want jobs with responsibility. This is true even for women with children. Many women still have some concern about balancing work and life. Men increasingly have similar concerns. Overall, women and men are often reporting the same goals and concerns. Younger people in particular are more open to changing gender roles that provide for more equality between the sexes. Katherine Lewis is a writer and editor focused on money, work, and family.

"How Gender Roles Are Changing in the U.S.," by Katherine Lewis, Dotdash Publishing Family, December 1, 2018. Reprinted by permission.

As you read, consider the following questions:

1. How do the views of younger people compare to those of older people, according to the survey?
2. How do women and men differ in their reports of who does housework and cleaning?
3. How have men's views changed in recent decades, according to the research?

Gender roles are changing at work and at home, according to the research done at the Families and Work Institute in 2008 (revised in 2011, the most recent at publication time). Young men and women alike are challenging traditional gender roles and expecting to share in paid work, as well as tending the household and children according to the benchmark survey of 3,500 Americans.

Converging Gender Roles

For the first time in the survey's history, it showed that women under 29 years of age are just as likely as men to want jobs with more responsibility.

In 1992, the survey found 80 percent of men under 29 years of age wanted jobs with more responsibility, compared to 72 percent of young women. The desire for more responsibility decreased for both genders in the 1997 survey (to 61 percent for men and 54 percent for women), and then went up in 2002 to 66 percent for men and 56 percent for women.

In 2008, the young women who did not want more responsibility explained why:

- 31 percent cited increased job pressure.
- 19 percent already have a high-level job.
- 15 percent expressed concern about having enough flexibility to manage work and home.

Motherhood Doesn't Dim Ambition

The second trend the researchers highlighted was that in the 2008 survey, young mothers wanted more job responsibility than their peers who had no children.

Looking at women under 29 in 1992, 78 percent of childless women versus 60 percent of mothers wanted more responsibility. That flip-flopped in 2008, with only 66 percent of child-free woman and 69 percent of young mothers wanting higher-responsibility jobs.

"In comparing 1992 with 2008, two emerging trends are striking: among millennials (under 29 years old), women are just as likely as men to want jobs with greater responsibility," the report said. "Today, there is no difference between young women with and without children in their desire to move to jobs with more responsibility."

"Taken together, these two trends suggest that millennial women are on a similar footing with their male colleagues when it comes to career ambitions and expectation," the report said.

Men and Women Agree on Gender Roles

Also, for the first time in the survey's history, in 2008 roughly the same percentage of men and women believed in traditional gender roles.

About 42 percent of men and 39 percent of women agreed with the statement that it's better for everyone "if the man earns the money and the woman takes care of the home and children." That's down from 74 percent of men and 52 percent of women who supported traditional gender roles in 1977.

You'll notice that more men than women have shifted their views on gender roles between 1977 and 2008. Men in dual-earning households changed their attitudes the most, with only 37 percent holding traditional views in 2008 versus 70 percent in 1977.

Older generations historically hold more traditional views on gender than young people. But the report found members of older generations being more open to non-traditional gender roles than in the past.

More Acceptance of Working Moms

In 2008, 73 percent of employees said working mothers can have as good of a relationship with their children as stay-at-home moms. That's up from 58 percent in 1977.

Among men, the figure was 67 percent in 2008 and 49 percent in 1977. For women, 80 percent in 2008 believed working moms can have equally good child relationships, up from 71 percent in 1977.

People who grew up with a working mom were more likely to strongly agree that working mothers can have just as good relationships with children.

Who Does the Chores?

In 2008, 56 percent of men said they did at least half the cooking, up from 34 percent in 1992. Wives see it slightly differently though with only 25 percent saying men do at least half, up from 15 percent in 1992.

As for house cleaning, there's an even greater difference of perception about who does the work. Fifty-three percent of men said they do at least half, up from 40 percent in 1992. But only 20 percent of women said their spouse does at least half, up from 18 percent in 1992, not a statistically significant difference.

"It has clearly become more socially acceptable for men to be and to say they are involved in child care, cooking and cleaning over the past three decades than it was in the past," the report said.

Growing Work-Life Conflict for Men

As fathers and husbands increase their responsibilities at home, they're also experiencing more difficulty balancing work and family duties.

In 2008, 45 percent of men reported feeling work-life conflict, up from 34 percent in 1997. That compares with 39 percent of women feeling the conflict in 2008, up from 34 percent in 1997.

Fathers were hit the hardest, with 59 percent of dads in dual-earner households reporting work-family conflict, versus

35 percent in 1977. In single-earner families, 50 percent of fathers felt the conflict.

Looking at moms, 45 percent felt the conflict in 2008, up from 41 percent in 1977.

It's great to see that gender roles continue to alter but there is still much work to be done to better our working mom culture.

"Much of the objection to change in gender roles is really about gender and power, not just about gender."

Equality Remains Distant Because Men Resist Losing Power

Laura Liswood

The previous viewpoint looked at survey responses about gender from the United States. In the following viewpoint Laura Liswood of the World Economic Forum explores gender parity, or equality, around the world. The World Economic Forum is an international organization that brings together political, business, and other leaders of society. The organization estimates that gender parity is a long way off. In fact, the move toward gender equality is slowing down. The author explores one reason for this trend: unconscious bias. Equality can seem unfair to those in power, because they lose their advantages. She argues that men may be open to equality in theory, but they fight against the loss of their own power. Laura Liswood is secretary-general of the Council of Women World Leaders for the World Economic Forum.

"Here's Why Gender Equality Is Taking So Long," by Laura Liswood, World Economic Forum, September 20, 2017. Reprinted by permission.

As you read, consider the following questions:

1. What is unconscious bias?
2. How do men feel when women get equal attention, according to research reported in the viewpoint?
3. How do men's changing roles in society sometimes lead to a backlash against women, according to the viewpoint?

The World Economic Forum estimates gender parity globally may now be over 170 years away. Previously they estimated an 80-year time, then it was 120 years. It keeps slowing down. The Forum's Annual Gender Gap Report shows slow progress and minimal change in many countries worldwide. What is causing this glacial pace of change, something the airline industry calls a "creeping delay"?

There are many headwinds that can lengthen the time required for desired systemic change, but there is one I'd like to address here, head on, and it's this: unconscious bias.

In general, there is a lack of awareness about who others are and what their capabilities and inherent qualities may be. In corporations, this often manifests as a culture that is unfriendly or unhelpful to women.

It's All About Power

What is unconscious bias? It can include anything from the preferences and perspectives we hold to the associations, roles and behaviours we carry out. A large part of it may be down to unconscious grievance and loss.

A "manifesto" written by a male Google employee this summer is a case in point. He posited that there are inherent psychological differences between men and women which lead to a disparity in how successful they are in the world of tech. It's clear that this man, and many like him, see diversity as eroding meritocracy and destroying the level playing field.

It is not my place to question whether Google was correct in firing him; he had his point to make. But I will say that whether he knows it or not, he is unconsciously finding selective arguments to resist change. He has something to lose.

The Google manifesto reflected this employee's belief that everyone lives in the same world as he does. But his is not a universal experience. He is unlikely to have been subject to systematic interruptions and the repeated questioning of his credentials or capabilities. He probably wasn't assumed to be incompetent until he proved otherwise, or excluded from informal mentoring or "bro" bonding. It's doubtful his comments were seen as aggressive rather than assertive, and that he was seldom acknowledged or taken seriously.

It's true the young engineer may have had some of this happen to him; but statistically, as a white male, he would not have experienced it at the same level or intensity as his female colleagues, nor felt its cumulative impact. He is unaware of the subtle advantages and perceived abilities "naturally" attributed to him. He may not truly grasp that for many women, their lack of success can be explained in part by the less-than-level playing field they work in. If it is made truly level, he will lose that subtle advantage he doesn't even see. The presence of capable women threatens the norms he has become used to.

When Equality Equals Loss

I believe there is a need to look closely at the loss and grievance that the dominant group feels when those from the non-dominant groups start to encroach on their societal position. In her book *Why So Slow*, Virginia Valerian found that while men can embrace the need for efforts that lead to fairness, such as equal pay, they have a much harder time with their own loss of centrality. This is about entitlement and holding a privileged place in the home, at work and in society. The loss of that privilege is a severe grievance.

For example, it is accurate to state that manufacturing jobs are diminishing and care jobs are in demand. It is quite another to have men accept new gender roles that they find emasculating. One survey focused in Middle Eastern and North African countries found that men harass women in public "to put them in their place." Much of the objection to change in gender roles is really about gender and power, not just about gender.

Joan C. Williams reflects on changing gender roles in her book *White Working Class: Overcoming Class Cluelessness in America*. She talks about "good" men and "real" men. The former are supportive, empathetic, collaborative. The latter are men who work in clearly identified masculine jobs, are assertive, take leadership at home and at work.

If we ask men to change their definitions of themselves it is not surprising that many will resist and find reasons to be critical of those they perceive as forcing this change upon them.

Geena Davis, at her eponymous media institute, has found that when a room's population is 20% women, men see 50%. When it is 30%, men feel it as 60%. The American Council on Education did a study asking teachers to call on boys and girls as best they could 50/50. After the experiment, the boys were asked how it felt. Their common response was: "The girls were getting all the attention." The boys (and men) feel a loss when equality is achieved. They have normalised overbalance.

As digital technology brings about massive global change, the World Economic Forum, which calls this shift the Fourth Industrial Revolution, is working to ready society for the upcoming disruptions. But for some, moving from a gendered position will feel like a loss, even though the shift may ironically reflect a more equal society.

> "*Women ... don't just face glass ceilings to advancement, they also are also 'stuck' to domestic life by endless chores.*"

The Media Reinforces Sexist Gender Roles

Virginia García Beaudoux

In the following viewpoint, Virginia García Beaudoux discusses the portrayal of women in film and TV. She notes that many advertisements encourage traditional gender roles. In particular, women are more often shown doing domestic chores, such as cleaning. She argues that this reinforces the idea that housework is women's work. Statistics show that women do in fact spend far more time on housework than men do. Yet, the author argues, changing what people see in the media could help change gender expectations in real life. Virginia García Beaudoux is a professor at two universities in Argentina. She teaches, writes about, and lectures internationally on politics, leadership, and gender.

As you read, consider the following questions:

1. How does the advertising industry target customers based on traditional gender roles, according to the viewpoint?
2. How is the United Kingdom responding to gender stereotypes in advertising?
3. How does the portrayal of women in advertising have real-world consequences, according to the author?

The sexual abuse scandal currently embroiling media mogul Harvey Weinstein has stunned the United States, with Hollywood and the fashion industry declaring that "this way of treating women ends now."

As an Argentinean woman who studies gender in the media, I find it hard to be surprised by Weinstein's misdeeds. Machismo remains deeply ingrained in Latin American society, yes, but even female political leaders in supposedly gender-equal paradises like Holland and Sweden have told me that they are criticized more in the press and held to a higher standard than their male counterparts.

How could they not be? Across the world, the film and TV industry—Weinstein's domain—continues to foist outdated gender roles upon viewers.

Women's Work

Television commercials are particularly guilty, frequently casting women in subservient domestic roles.

Take this 2015 ad for the Argentine cleaning product Cif, which is still running today. It explains how its concentrated cleaning capsules "made Sleeping Beauty shine."

In it, a princess eager to receive her prince remembers that—gasp—the floors in her castle tower are a total mess. Thanks to Cif's magic scouring fluid, she has time not only to clean but also to get dolled up for the prince—who, in case you were wondering, has no physical challenges preventing him from helping her tidy up.

But why should he, when it's a woman's job to be both housekeeper and pretty princess?

Somewhat paradoxically, advertisements may also cast men as domestic superheroes. Often, characters like Mr. Muscle will mansplain to women about the best product and how to use it— though they don't actually do any cleaning themselves.

More recently, there's been a shift—perhaps an awkward attempt at political correctness—in which women are still the masters of the home, but their partners are shown "helping out" with the chores. In exchange, the men earn sex object status.

We've Come a Little Way, Baby

Various studies on gender stereotypes in commercials indicate that although the advertising industry is slowly changing for the better, marketing continues to target specific products to certain customers based on traditional gender roles.

Women are pitched hygiene and cleaning products, whereas men get ads for banks, credit cards, housing, cars and other significant financial investments.

This year, U.N. Women teamed up with Unilever and other industry leaders like Facebook, Google, Mars and Microsoft to launch the Unstereotype Alliance. The aim of this global campaign is to end stereotypical and sexist portrayals of gender in advertising.

As part of the #Unstereotype campaign, Unilever also undertook research on gender in advertising. It found that only 3 percent of advertising shows women as leaders and just 2 percent conveys them as intelligent. In ads, women come off as interesting people just 1 percent of the time.

Britain Paves a Path

Even before it was forced to reckon with allegations that Harvey Weinstein had also harassed women in London, the United Kingdom was making political progress on the issue of women's portrayal in the media.

In July, the United Kingdom's Advertising Standards Authority announced that the U.K. will soon prohibit commercials that promote gender stereotypes.

"While advertising is only one of many factors that contribute to unequal gender outcomes," its press release stated, "tougher advertising standards can play an important role in tackling inequalities and improving outcomes for individuals, the economy and society as a whole."

As of 2018, the agency says, advertisements in which women are shown as solely responsible for household cleaning or men appear useless around kitchen appliances and unable to handle taking care of their children and dependents will not pass muster in the U.K. Commercials that differentiate between girls' and boys' toys based on gender stereotypeswill be banned as well.

Sticky Floors

The U.K.'s move is a heartening public recognition that gender stereotypes in the media both reflect and further the very real inequalities women face at home and at work.

Worldwide, the International Labor Organization reports, women still bear the burden of household chores and caretaking responsibilities, which often either excludes them from pay work or leaves them relegated to ill-paid part-time jobs.

In the U.K., men spend on average 16 hours per week on domestic tasks, while women spend 26. The European Union average is worse, with women dedicating an average of 26 weekly hours to men's nine hours on caretaking and household tasks.

In Argentina, my home country, fully 40 percent of men report doing no household work at all, even if they're unemployed. Among those who do pitch in, it's 24 hours a week on caretaking and domestic chores for men. Argentinean women put in 45 hours.

You can do the math: On average, Argentinean women use up two days of their week and some 100 days annually—nearly one-third of their year—on unpaid household labor.

Real-World Consequences

These inequalities, combined with advertising that reinforces them, generate what's called the "sticky floors" problem. Women—whether would-be investment bankers or, I dare say, aspiring Hollywood stars—don't just face glass ceilings to advancement, they also are also "stuck" to domestic life by endless chores.

The cultural powers that be produce content that represents private spaces as "naturally" imbued with female qualities, gluing women to traditional caregiving roles.

This hampers their professional development and helps keep them at the bottom of the economy pyramid because women must pull off a balancing act between their jobs inside and outside of the domestic sphere. And they must excel at both, all while competing against male colleagues who likely confront no such challenges.

Former U.S. president Barack Obama once pointed out this double standard in homage to his then-competitor Hillary Clinton. She, he reminded an audience in 2008, "was doing everything I was doing, but just like Ginger Rogers, it was backwards in heels."

The sticky floor problem puts women in a position to be exploited by men like Weinstein, who tout their ability to help female aspirants to get unstuck. Until society—and, with it, the media we create—comprehend that neither professional success nor domesticity has a gender, these pernicious powerful dynamics will endure.

> *"If dying young is common, it affects people's economic decisions."*

Culture Determines Whether More Men or Women Survive

Prabir Bhattacharya

In the following viewpoint, Prabir Bhattacharya addresses gender ratios around the world. He notes that typically, slightly more boy babies than girl babies are born. Yet males die more quickly than females, which can lead to a much greater number of elderly women than elderly men. In India, China, and South Korea social standards favor males. This leads some parents to abort female fetuses or take less care of girl children. The author argues that girls have a better chance of survival when women have greater rights and opportunities. Therefore, the economy plays a part in the sex ratio and so does gender equality. Prabir Bhattacharya is an associate professor of economics at Heriot-Watt University based in Scotland.

As you read, consider the following questions:

1. What is meant by the "human sex ratio"?
2. How can this ratio change as people age?
3. How do gender-based opportunities affect the number of females and males who survive to old age?

"What You Can Tell About a Country's Future by Looking at Its Gender Balance," by Prabir Bhattacharya, The Conversation, 08/28/2014. http://theconversation.com/what-you-can-tell-about-a-countrys-future-by-looking-at-its-gender-balance-30987. Licensed under CC BY 4.0 International.

The human sex ratio, which is usually defined in terms of the number of males per 100 females, varies greatly between countries and regions. The biological norm is for the sex ratio at birth to be about 105 more or less everywhere—meaning just over 51% of births are boys and just under 49% are girls.

But with equal care and feeding, females die less quickly. It is therefore not surprising that the sex ratio of the population as a whole in the West and in many other regions leans in favour of women. In the UK this ratio is 99; in the US, 97; and in the EU, 96. In sub-Saharan Africa, where life expectancy at birth for is relatively low for both sexes, the ratio is 99. In Russia, Ukraine and some former Eastern bloc countries, it is among the lowest in the world: 86 for both Russia and Ukraine.

Russia's Male Problem

There are other countries—notably China and India—where the ratio is abnormally high: the ratio is 106 in both countries. Yet even in India and China, there are now more elderly women than men. The sex ratio among over-65s is 90 in India and 91 in China. By comparison, it is 76 for the UK and 75 for the US. For Russia this ratio seems astonishingly low: only 45.

Couple this with the fact that the overall sex ratio is also quite low in Russia, yet the sex ratio at birth and for childhood years is in line with the international norm. The difference in life expectancy at birth between males and females in Russia is also 13 years in favour of females—the widest anywhere. It all suggests a problem of "missing men" in Russia (the reverse of the "missing women" problem in India and China).

Since 1992, Russia's population has declined by 7m from 149m to 142m. This decline is linked to high mortality rates and a sudden sharp decline in fertility. After the collapse of communism, the fertility rate plunged from 2.2 births per woman in 1987 to 1.17 in 1991 (the replacement level of fertility is 2.1). It has since recovered to around 1.3, but that is still among the lowest in the world. At the same time, the death rate went in the opposite direction. In

1991-92 it passed the birth rate and since then Russia has recorded nearly 13m more deaths than births.

This upsurge in mortality has been disproportionately concentrated among men and women of working age, particularly men. For men in their 30s and 40s, Russia's death rate today is roughly twice what it was 40 years ago. It has been estimated that if Russia had maintained the hardly-exacting survival rates of the years just before the collapse of communism, there would have been 6.6m fewer deaths between 1992 and 2006 (4.9m of them men).

Drowning in Vodka

While there have been rapid increases in HIV/AIDS infections and tuberculosis in Russia, the main causes of this mortality upsurge are deaths from heart disease and "external causes" such as injuries, homicide and suicide. Alcohol is the common denominator. Russian men in particular tend to consume hard spirits and to drink in binges.

It has been estimated that an average male adult drinks a bottle of vodka per week (or the equivalent). Russians have always drunk vodka, but the psychological stress following the collapse of communism would appear to have played an important role in recent times. One is tempted to say that a large number of Russians have lost the will to live and are simply drinking themselves to death.

But why have men of working age suffered more than women? It has been suggested that the gender order that developed during the Soviet era made men virtually redundant within the typical Russian household, especially in urban areas. It served the perceived needs of the state by expecting women to combine roles as workers, mothers and household managers; while men's far more limited role involved serving as soldiers, workers and managers.

Soviet society was "matrifocal" with everyday family life relying "heavily on cross-generational help and caregiving relations, taking place mostly between women", and men estranged from most family spheres. The respect men commanded within the household depended mainly on their role as primary breadwinners. Once that role came under threat or disappeared at the end of the Soviet era, they had no other roles or support network to fall back on. Since vodka drinking had always been part of traditional Russian male culture, it was the obvious culturally appropriate way for men to cope with their hardships.

The danger here is that if dying young is common, it affects people's economic decisions. They will be less likely to spend years acquiring training and education to benefit their future. Companies become less likely to invest in their workforces. People are less likely to save for their futures, which can become a drain on the state in years to come.

The India–China Comparison

Be that as it may, men are not dying in larger numbers than women in Russia because of any deliberate discrimination against them. In India and China, by contrast, the culture of discrimination against females has been mainly responsible for the sex-ratio imbalances. Both countries have a problem with sex-selective abortions and higher rates of female child mortailty.

Having said that, life expectancy at birth for both males and females has been increasing in both countries. The gains for females have been much greater than for males in the past few years, and overall female life expectancy now exceeds male life expectancy in both countries by about four years. This increase in female life expectancy is tilting the sex ratio away from its male bias.

South Korea may provide a precedent. Its sex ratio at birth was the highest in the world in 1990, peaking at 117 (54% boys). Only ten years earlier it had been normal—just at the point when sex-determination tests were becoming available and sex-selective abortions became possible. And in more recent years, the figures have returned to around the norm. Contributory factors are thought to include increased urbanisation; structural change in the economy from agriculture to non-agriculture; greater employment opportunities for women; greater prosperity for individuals; establishing more nuclear families and several laws giving special rights to women.

In India there are now signs that those states with the biggest male birth bias—Punjab and Haryana—are also beginning to reverse. But this has to be set against the fact that the sex ratio in the birth-to-six-years category in some states with less male birth bias has been increasing. In China, the sex ratio at birth did shift appreciably towards girls during 2000–05 in several regions such as the contiguous south-eastern provinces of Guandong, Hainan and Guangxi. In some other areas, the ratio has been stagnant.

Korea Opportunities?

It is possible that India and China will follow the South Korea path towards a more balanced sex ratio as their economies develop. High sex ratios at birth continue to be major problems, but rising life expectancy at birth for both males and females is encouraging: the gains have been strongest in the last few years, particularly for females. India also has the advantage that her youth ratio in the population is higher as compared to many other countries.

It is hard to avoid the conclusion that India and China probably have better prospects of sustained economic growth in the foreseeable future than Russia, where the situation continues to look gloomy. The old Soviet gender order is being actively maintained and binge vodka drinking continues to be part of traditional male culture. Death rates among working age people are still a problem. Male life expectancy is lower than in the late 1950s. Russia wishes to be a great economic and political power again. But surely an economy and society where human capital is as precariously poised as in Russia is likely to be greatly limited by that weakness.

> "*Watching Disney princesses waft about was associated with higher levels of female gender-stereotypical behaviour.*"

Break Gender Stereotypes Early

Tania King

In the following viewpoint Tania King argues that gender stereotyping should be tackled as early as preschool. The author notes that research has shown that young children are aware of gender differences and that books, toys, and media representation can all contribute to expectations of their gender roles. And while some of these stereotypes can result in positive outcomes, they are harmful in general. Tania King is a senior research fellow at the Melbourne School of Population and Global Health, Faculty of Medicine, Dentistry and Health, Sciences, University of Melbourne.

As you read, consider the following questions:

1. When does gender awareness arise in children?
2. Are toys divided by gender more or less than they were fifty years ago?
3. Should we disregard categories like boys and girls, according to the author?

We all know that children are like little detectives. They are constantly seeking to classify and categorise the world around them in order to make sense of it.

Part of a child's development is the process of beginning to understand, and grapple with, the complex concept of gender.

Recent media reports have highlighted that it doesn't matter how old you get—understanding gender, and all its associated misconceptions, judgements and assumptions—remains complex well into adulthood.

Despite reports to the contrary, Victorian councils are not planning to remove any children's books from library shelves under new gender guidelines informed by our research over the last few years.

In 2016, Associate Professor Naomi Priest from the Australian National University and myself were commissioned by the City of Melbourne to conduct a literature review, to bring together evidence related to gender stereotypes in preschool children.

And while this is an area where theory abounds, we found that there was a lack of empirical, or hard, evidence about the influences on children's perception of gender.

It's now fairly well-established that awareness of gender emerges early in a child's life—this is nothing new. It's also clear that awareness of gender stereotypes arises early in life too.

Research done in 2007 among three to five-year-olds found that at an early age, these kids were able to identify "girl toys" and "boy toys"—and predict whether their parents would approve or disapprove of their choice. In 2011, an American study of children aged between six and 10-years-old found that the stereotype that "maths is for boys" starts quite young.

But much of the research we looked at showed us that there are many things that influence children's establishment of gender norms and stereotypes. Some of these things we do without thinking can have a big impact—like switching on the TV.

FACING STIGMA AS A NONBINARY PERSON

Gender is a topic that is being discussed more widely in general, and recognition of concepts such as nonbinary gender is also increasing. Nonbinary people may, therefore, be more recognized and accepted than in years past, but nonbinary gender is still often viewed as "different" or outside of what is "normal" by many people. A gender binary is often assumed by many people, leading nonbinary individuals to often be viewed with skepticism and doubt.

Those who identify as nonbinary often experience a type of coming-out process when sharing their gender identity with others. They may be subjected to embarrassing questions from those who do not understand their experience. Individuals who identify as nonbinary may also feel their gender identity is not validated, as people sometimes inquire whether a certain gender category really exists or whether nonbinary people are just trying to be different. Society's significant bias toward a binary understanding of gender can also cause feelings of distress and dysphoria and otherwise lead individuals to feel as if they are not recognized, accepted, or understood. For example, many forms that ask about gender require a person to indicate whether they are male or female but provide no option for individuals who have a different gender identity.

TV, Toys and Kids

One study we looked at found that the more TV children of both sexes watched, the more likely they were to believe that "boys are better." For little boys, watching television appears to reinforce their already positive self-regard, while for girls, watching television appears to dampen it.

This is concerning given that there are more than twice as many male characters as there are female characters on kid's TV shows.

But the type of TV shows our kids are watching can also have an influence on the type of play that they engage in: boys watching violent and superhero programs were more likely to play in gender stereotyped games; and for both boys and girls, watching Disney

The stigma that exists around nonbinary gender identity, and the prejudice and discrimination many face, can be difficult to deal with, potentially painful, and may contribute to mental health and emotional concerns.

People who are gender-nonconforming may be at increased risk for depression, anxiety, substance use, and victimization. While the stigma associated with a nonbinary gender identity may present many challenges, people often still experience a sense of relief once they are able to be open about their experience of gender and have the words to describe it. Knowing the term nonbinary exists to describe gender identity that doesn't fit into a binary system helps many people who do not identify as exclusively male or female feel validated and understood.

New terms such as pronouns may seem unfamiliar at first, and some people may find it difficult to adjust their perspective of a person they have known for years. However, recognizing a person's pronouns and identity, and accepting gender as a spectrum rather than a binary, is the best way to show them support, and doing so can help increase acceptance and reduce stigma and prejudice.

"Nonbinary Gender," GoodTherapy, LLC.

princesses waft about was associated with higher levels of female gender-stereotypical behaviour.

Relatedly, there is also evidence toys are now more divided by gender than they were 50 years ago. What is concerning about this, is that certain types of toys like Lego and other construction toys typically marketed to boys, are thought to build skills that help mathematical reasoning.

According to some, this may underpin the under-representation of women in maths and science. One minister in the UK said that "toys marketed to boys boosted interest in science and maths" and in the process, girls are discouraged from taking up maths and engineering jobs.

While there's no specific research examining the relationship between toys and outcomes for boys, it's important to note that stereotypes can work against boys as well as girls.

For example, one study among early childhood teachers in Spain showed many perceived girls as more caring and helpful than boys, and indeed, teachers expected this behaviour from girls. But boys exhibiting prosocial behaviour like this were considered surprising—even sometimes strange.

Meanwhile in Australia

But what about geographical or cultural context?

What is found in one country or context may not be necessarily applicable to us here in Australia. Most research of this type has been conducted in the US, and little research has been conducted domestically.

However, we only have to visit the toy section in many of our shops to see how gender delineated toys, and play, has become.

But the process of categorisation isn't one we can easily get way from. It's an essential element of the human need to make sense of our world. It's when these categories are then assigned rigid stereotypes, attitudes or beliefs about roles, behaviours or even worth, that they become problematic.

We can never remove terms and categories that are a normal part of life such as "boys" and "girls," nor should we.

However, research does suggest that by minimising these distinctions on the basis of gender and making individual attributes and skills a priority, we can help reduce stereotypes, discrimination and bias, and instead, build inclusive behaviours in our children.

> *"Identifying as nonbinary is a fix for the individual, not for the whole, and I'm not sure how, in the long run, that helps anyone."*

A Nonbinary Future Erases Women

Katie Herzog

In the following viewpoint Katie Herzog explores the impact of a nonbinary future on women. Some people believe that modern society should pay less attention to gender. The author warns that this could have unfortunate repercussions. She suggests that identifying as nonbinary allows people to remove themselves from the gender hierarchy. However, it does not help dismantle that hierarchy. Therefore, a nonbinary future erases the concerns of women and in particular lesbians. Embracing a nonbinary future reinforces gender stereotypes. The author claims that everyone has elements of the masculine and the feminine, but that does not make people nonbinary. Katie Herzog is a staff writer at the Stranger, *a Seattle newspaper.*

"If the Future Is Nonbinary, It's a Bleak One for Women," by Katie Herzog, The Stranger, Index Newspapers LLC, November 30, 2018. Reprinted by permission.

As you read, consider the following questions:

1. What are some advantages that nonbinary people may get, according to the author?
2. How would a nonbinary future erase women, according to the viewpoint?
3. How would a nonbinary future reinforce gender stereotypes, in the author's view?

I n the beginning, the future was female.

This four-word slogan started popping up online in the last few years, but it originated with a snapshot taken by Liza Cowan in 1975. The photo, which has gone viral many times over on Instagram, shows Cowan's then-girlfriend, a folk singer named Alix Dobkin, with short hair, red-framed glasses, and a white t-shirt that read, in all caps, "THE FUTURE IS FEMALE." According to the *New York Times*, the shirt was designed for Labyris Books, the first women's bookstore in New York City, and Cowan titled her photo, "What The Well-Dressed Dyke Will Wear."

Dobkin is now in her late 70s and Labyris long ago closed, but in the heady days before the election of November 2016, the photo, and the slogan, were everywhere. Hillary Clinton even used it on the campaign trail. Naturally, companies noticed. "The Future Is Female" was repurposed by the apparel store Otherwild, which started selling its own version of the shirt for $50 and donating a portion of sales to Planned Parenthood.

The shirt was a hit, photographed on contemporary tastemakers like Kelly Rowland, Annie Clark (the musician behind St. Vincent), and her then-model girlfriend Cara Delevingne. It spread to bracelets, calendars, cards, tote bags, onesies, and anything else you can print with four words and mark up. There are now knock-off Future Is Female shirts you can get online for much less than Otherwild sells them—no donation to Planned Parenthood required. Or, for a more bespoke version, just search on Etsy, and you'll find over 6,000 Future Is Female products to choose from.

Despite the slogan's popularity, "The Future Is Female" is not without its critics. Originally, the slogan was a nod to dyke culture, lesbian separatism, and a future without men. In the intersectional politics du jour, however, the slogan was eventually deemed exclusionary. This was not because the slogan excludes men (who cares about them) but because the concept of female itself has, in some circles, been deemed problematic.

On Tuesday, *Rewire News* published an opinion piece called, "No, the Future Is Not Female. It's Nonbinary." Written by Jessica Porten, a self-identified "white heterosexual woman who was assigned female at birth and has birthed two children," Porten writes, "The word 'female' is still invoked as the scientific definition of a biological woman, which incorrectly conflates sex and gender and erases the identities of intersex and nonbinary people. ... I am not saying everyone should or will eventually identify as nonbinary. But the future is one where we don't push a binary norm. The future should be nonbinary," she concludes. "Period."

There is, however, a big difference between intersex and nonbinary. The term "intersex" describes a variety of medical conditions, usually stemming from a genetic anomaly. Some intersex people are born with ambiguous genitalia, like a micropenis or an atypically large clit[oris]. Others are born without the usual pairing of XX or XY chromosomes.

For much of modern history, people with these conditions have been forced to undergo surgery to "correct" the appearance of their genitals, often when they are infants and without their consent. After years of activism on the part of people with intersex conditions, however, "normalizing" genitals through surgery is no longer as common. Intersex people born now are often free to grow up with their junk intact. Some elect to have surgery later, and others don't.

Nonbinary, however, is something entirely different, and the two should also not be conflated. It's not a medical condition or a genetic anomaly and, with the rare exception of people raising "theybies," or gender-neutral children, it's not something, generally speaking, people are born with. Some intersex people are themselves nonbinary, but the concept is about gender identity, not sex. It's a label, one that says, "I'm not a man or a woman. I'm something else."

Motivations for identifying as nonbinary vary: Some nonbinary people (or enbies, as they are called) report that they have a feeling deep inside of being neither male nor female—or, alternatively, of being both. This feeling is not necessarily gender dysphoria, and while some transgender people are nonbinary, there are many (perhaps more) trans people who readily identify as men or women. Some enbies are androgynous or bounce between looks, and others are assigned male at birth and present masculine and others are assigned female at birth who present feminine. Writer Peter Coffin, for instance—a bearded father of two who is married to a feminine-presenting woman—came out earlier this year as "agender," a subsidiary of the nonbinary identity. Why? Because, in his own words, he "disliked [his] place in the gender dynamic." So, instead of working to dismantle a hierarchy that places men at the top and women at the bottom, he simply stopped identifying as a man, while, of course, still receiving all the privileges of people who look like them. I suppose that's one way to deal with structural sexism.

While there's been no comprehensive census of people calling themselves nonbinary (much less agender), gray-bearded fathers like Peter Coffin, are, from my observation, the minority. Far more common are people like Sam Escobar, a 20-something assigned-female-at-birth (née woman) and deputy director at Allure who uses the pronouns they/them. Escobar described their journey to becoming an enby for *Esquire*.

"I only began investigating my curiosity when I got to college," they write. "After hours of combing through message boards and LGBTQ-centric sites, I realized that on top of being queer, I identified considerably with men. It had nothing to do sports, beer, or bro hugs. To be frank, I realized that, among other things, when I watched straight porn I saw myself from the male perspective."

After this revelation, Escobar writes that they bought a binder for their chest, started applying their makeup in a more androgynous fashion, and considered cutting their hair, though ultimately didn't. Years later, now out of college and living in New York in a community of queer people of all genders and identities, they publicly came out on Facebook, writing, they say, "I identify as queer and nonbinary. I prefer they and them pronouns. This is me coming out." They've got plenty of company: According to a GLAAD study from last year, 20 percent of millennials identify as LGBTQ; 12 percent identify as trans or otherwise gender nonconforming. It's hip to be queer. It's even hipper to be nonbinary. (And I will almost certainly be accused of enbyphobia for pointing this out.)

One of the great things about living in a free society is that we are able to, largely, do as we please, as long as our doing doesn't harm anyone else. I'd much rather live in a society where people like Coffin and Escobar are able to freely experiment with identity (or fashion, which often seems to be the same thing) than someplace without that same freedom. I don't want to denigrate any individual's identity, a concept that has taken on near religious status as of late, and I generally believe adults should do and call themselves whatever they want. But for every article or Tumblr post celebrating nonbinary identities and inclusion, there's a real lack of discussion on what the rise of the nonbinary identity means for those who actually identify as, who actually are, just women.

In its effort to be inclusive, "The Future Is Nonbinary" (now also available as a t-shirt) does exactly the same thing that Porten complains about: It erases a population. In this case, the population is women, both cis and trans. Perhaps ironically, it seems to be mostly young women doing the erasing, and when our news feeds are filled with stories of women being harassed, assaulted, and oppressed, it's not hard to see why they'd reject being a woman at all. Women, in much of the are world are on the bottom of the hierarchy. Who wouldn't want to get out from that? Identifying as nonbinary can be a way of creating your own exemption. It is, perhaps, ironic that trend is ballooning mostly in the U.S. and other egalitarian societies instead of, say, Saudia Arabia, where women need a man's permission to do much of anything. (Then again, in places where women are legally second-class, you probably can't opt out of being one.)

Enbies have some privileges women don't. Take Instagram, one of many platforms where women are not permitted to show their nipples. If, however, those same nipples are on a nonbinary person, it's totally fine. Instagram will leave those nipples up. Personally, Instagram's ban on women's nipples doesn't impact my lifestyle all that much, but it's about more than that. It's about equal treatment and double standards, and if men and nonbinary people can go topless, why the hell can't women, too? As Rain Dove, a nonbinary model permitted to post topless pics on Instagram shows, they're often the the very same tits.

"We all have moral and ethical obligations to decolonize our thoughts and language, rooting out binaries that label and devalue people," Porten writes in Rewire. But she neglects that the term "nonbinary" often ignores the broad spectrum of interests, abilities, and emotions of women and men alike. Instead of broadening our concepts of what men and women can be and do—instead of saying a woman can fix cars and man can wear makeup and they can still be women and men—the nonbinary identity throws everyone else under the gender-role bus. Identifying as nonbinary is a fix for the individual, not for the whole, and I'm not sure how, in the long run, that helps anyone.

Besides, the original slogan was not just about women. It was about gay women, another population that has rapidly been erased. Lesbian bars and bookstores and cafes are closing. Half of the lesbians I knew in the early 2000s are now either nonbinary or transmen. And Porten, who, according to her own admission, is heterosexual, is arguing that an ode to dyke culture should be supplanted by one that centers people who have rejected the concept of women. It's hard to see what's so progressive about that.

Now, I don't think "The Future Is Female" is a particularly appropriate slogan for this moment in time either. (Someone gave me a cheap version of the t-shirt and now it's a rag.) The slogan made sense in the '70s when lesbians like Cowan and Dobkin were still anathema and women more broadly were still emerging from decades in which their best options for a career were maid, secretary, teacher, nurse, or a wife. Women still did all the housework and raised all the kids. "The Future Is Female," at that time, was a radical statement about women's lib. Now, it's just an easy way to advertise your feminist bonafides. It's a t-shirt you can buy off Amazon, a credit card but no liberation required. Still, "The Future Is Nonbinary" is equally empty. It might look good on Instagram, but all it does is reenforce gender stereotypes. The reality is, we all have elements of both the masculine and the feminine. This doesn't make you binary or nonbinary. It makes you a human.

Periodical and Internet Sources Bibliography

The following articles have been selected to supplement the diverse views presented in this chapter.

Beaudoux, Virginia Garcia, "Success has no gender, so the media and society need to change," World Economic Forum, Oct 25, 2017. https://www.weforum.org/agenda/2017/10/success-has-no-gender-so-the-media-and-society-need-to-change

Cieslik, Anna, "The future is fluid: Generation Z's approach to gender and sexuality is indeed revolutionary," Daily Dot, Oct 18, 2017. https://www.dailydot.com/irl/generation-z-fluid/

"Consumers say gender roles have changed. Why hasn't advertising?" Retail Wire, Mar 16, 2018. https://www.retailwire.com/discussion/consumers-say-gender-roles-have-changed-why-hasnt-advertising/

Gokhale, Amar and Nitin Agarwal, "Future of Gender Equality: India in 2050," BWDISRUPT, Jun 4, 2017. http://bwdisrupt.businessworld.in/article/Future-of-Gender-Equality-India-in-2050/04-06-2017-119454/

Hayton, Debbie, "Open Future: Gender identity needs to be based on objective evidence rather than feelings," *Economist*, July 3rd 2018. https://www.economist.com/open-future/2018/07/03/gender-identity-needs-to-be-based-on-objective-evidence-rather-than-feelings

King, Tania, "Breaking Gender Stereotypes. Early," The University of Melbourne Pursuit. https://pursuit.unimelb.edu.au/articles/breaking-gender-stereotypes-early

Raskoff, Sally, "The Future of Gender?" Everyday Sociology, Jun 4, 2018. https://www.everydaysociologyblog.com/2018/06/the-future-of-gender.html

Shah, Ruan, "Why Gender Neutral Parenting Shouldn't Exist," Jerrick Media. https://families.media/why-gender-neutral-parenting-shouldnt-exist

Sumano, Karina, "How Gender Stereotypes Impact Behavior," One Love Foundation. https://www.joinonelove.org/learn/gender-stereotypes-impact-behavior/

For Further Discussion

Chapter 1

1. The viewpoints in this chapter address gender from several perspectives, including historical, biological, and sociological. Is one angle more accurate or important than the others? Why or why not? Can they all be reconciled? Explain.
2. John Hawkins argues that gender is not a social construct. He calls that concept dumb and his opponents stupid. How does his language support or detract from his claims? Are you more likely to agree or disagree with someone who is extremely critical? Why?
3. Tara Culp-Ressler suggests that strict gender roles are bad for mental health. Compare the experiences of the teens in the study to your own experiences. What similarities or differences do you see? Would you like to see changes in your community? How might that happen?

Chapter 2

1. What does it mean to be female, and what does it mean to be feminine? How are these aspects different? How are they connected?
2. Has society shifted so that gender bias is no longer an issue? Do women and men both suffer from stereotypes and bias? Why or why not?
3. Is there still a need for feminism? Does the country or culture under discussion make a difference? Explain.

Chapter 3

1. What does it mean to be male, and what does it mean to be masculine? How are these aspects different? How are they connected?

2. Is trying to change toxic masculinity the same as setting out to emasculate men? Explain your reasoning

3. How might you envision a new version of masculinity based on the viewpoints in this chapter? Explain.

Chapter 4

1. Katherine Lewis suggests that society is letting go of strict gender roles. Younger generations are less concerned about appearing masculine or feminine. How might a person's age influence their views on gender? Is this good, bad, or neutral? Explain your answer.

2. Laura Liswood argues that men in power see equality as unfair. Does her explanation make sense? Why or why not? If she's right, how might this affect the future of gender?

3. Some viewpoints in this book promote the idea of a gender-neutral or nonbinary future. Katie Herzog warns that this could harm women. Does she provide enough evidence to support that opinion? Explain your answer.

Organizations to Contact

The editors have compiled the following list of organizations concerned with the issues debated in this book. The descriptions are derived from materials provided by the organizations. All have publications or information available for interested readers. The list was compiled on the date of publication of the present volume; the information provided here may change. Be aware that many organizations take several weeks or longer to respond to inquiries, so allow as much time as possible.

American Men's Studies Association

1080 S. University Avenue
Ann Arbor, Michigan 48109-1106
(470) 333-AMSA
email: amsamail@gmail.com
website: mensstudies.org/

This academic organization is dedicated to studying men and masculinity. The group holds an annual conference and publishes the *Journal of Men's Studies*.

The Body Is Not an Apology (TBINAA)

Contact form: https://thebodyisnotanapology.com/about-tbinaa/contact-us/
website: thebodyisnotanapology.com/

TBINAA is an international movement "committed to cultivating global Radical Self-Love and Body Empowerment." Essays discuss racial justice, gender, LGBTQ/queer issues, disabilities, body image, and other topics.

Equality Now

125 Maiden Lane, 9th Floor, Suite B
New York NY 10038
(212) 586-0906
email: info@equalitynow.org
website: www.equalitynow.org/

Equality Now's goal is to eliminate violence and discrimination against women and girls around the world. It focuses on legal action. The website has publications and fact sheets.

The Good Men Project

email: info@goodmenproject.com
website: goodmenproject.com/about/

The Good Men Project is an international conversation about what it means to be a good man in the twenty-first century. Members can access classes, weekly calls, and groups. The website provides articles on sex and relationships, dads and families, sports, and advice.

The National Center for Men

117 Pauls Path #531
Coram, NY 11727
(631) 476-2115
contact form: www.nationalcenterformen.org/contactform. shtml
website: www.nationalcenterformen.org/

This group addresses many men's issues, from homelessness and rape to parenthood and child custody. Men can sign up for phone counseling, for a fee, through the website.

National Coalition For Men (NCFM)

932 C Street, Suite B
San Diego, CA 92101
email: ncfm@ncfm.org
website: ncfm.org/

Since 1977 NCFM "has been dedicated to the removal of harmful gender based stereotypes especially as they impact boys, men, their families and the women who love them." Issues pages on the website cover fathers, education, male rape victims, health, and more.

National Organization for Men Against Sexism

3500 E. 17th Avenue
Denver CO, 80206
(303) 997-9581
email: info@nomas.org
website: http://nomas.org/

The National Organization for Men Against Sexism (NOMAS) is an activist organization supporting positive changes for men. The website provides resources, a reading list, and a blog. Task groups tackle men's health, fathering, ending violence, eliminating racism, and much more.

National Organization for Women (NOW)

1100 H Street NW, Suite 300
Washington, DC 20005
(202) 628-8669
email: https://now.org/about/contact-us
website: now.org

NOW is dedicated to women's rights. The grassroots group has hundreds of chapters around the country. It promotes the equal rights of all women and girls in all aspects of life. Get news and learn how you can get involved.

Northern Illinois University The Center for the Study of Women, Gender and Sexuality (CSWGS)

Reavis Hall, Room 103
DeKalb, IL 60115
(815) 753-1038
email: wgs@niu.edu
website: niu.edu/cswgs/

CSWGS offers a variety of college programs and explains how gender studies can benefit young people

OutRight Action International

80 Maiden Lane, Suite 1505
New York, NY 10038
(212) 430-6054
email: hello@outrightinternational.org
website: www.outrightinternational.org

OutRight Action International fights for human rights for LGBTIQ people everywhere. Learn about the key issues in LGBTIQ activism.

ProMundo

1367 Connecticut Ave NW
Washington, DC 20036
(202) 588-0060
email: contact@promundoglobal.org
website: promundoglobal.org

Promundo promotes gender justice and prevents violence by engaging men and boys in partnership with women and girls.

Rice University Center for the Study of Women, Gender, and Sexuality

6100 Main Street
Houston, TX 77005-1892
(713) 348-0000
email: cswgs@rice.edu
website: https://cswgs.rice.edu/

The Ccnter fosters interdisciplinary research and teaching that addresses women, gender, and sexuality. Learn about the academic program and read articles in the Feminist Forum.

Teaching Tolerance, Southern Poverty Law Center

403 Washington Avenue
Montgomery, AL 36104
(888) 414-7752
Contact form: https://www.tolerance.org/contact
website: www.tolerance.org/

Teaching Tolerance provides many classroom resources, magazines, and other publications. Webinars are available free online. Visit https://www.tolerance.org/classroom-resources/tolerance-lessons/ what-are-gender-stereotypes for exercises on understanding gender stereotypes.

University of Warwick Center for the Study of Women and Gender

Social Sciences Building, The University of Warwick
Coventry, CV4 7AL
United Kingdom
email directory: https://warwick.ac.uk/fac/soc/sociology/staff/
website: https://warwick.ac.uk/fac/soc/sociology/research/ centres/gender/

CSWG is a center of research and teaching in women's, gender, and feminist studies. Members of this British social sciences center have a broad range of research in women's, gender, and feminist studies.

White Ribbon

36 Eglinton Ave W, Suite 603
Toronto, ON M4R 1A1, Canada
(416) 920-6684
email: info@whiteribbon.ca
website: www.whiteribbon.ca

White Ribbon is a movement of men and boys working to end violence against women and girls, promote gender equity, healthy relationships, and a new vision of masculinity.

Bibliography of Books

Chimamanda Ngozi Adichie. *We Should All Be Feminists*. New York, NY: Anchor Books, 2015.

Becca Anderson. *The Book of Awesome Women: Boundary Breakers, Freedom Fighters, Sheroes and Female Firsts*. Miami, FL: Mango, 2017.

Stephanie Brill and Lisa Kenney. *The Transgender Teen*. Jersey City, NJ: Cleis Press, 2016.

Shannon N. Davis. Gender in the Twenty-First Century: The Stalled Revolution and the Road to Equality.: Berkeley, CA: University of California Press, 2017.

Dr. Joseph Gelfer. *Numen, Old Men: Contemporary Masculine Spiritualities and the Problem of Patriarchy*. Abingdon, United Kingdom: Routledge, 2009.

Bell Hooks. *Feminism Is for Everybody: Passionate Politics*. United Kingdom: Routledge, 2014.

Bell Hooks. *Yearning: Race, Gender, and Cultural Politics*. United Kingdom: Routledge, 2014.

Kelly Jensen. *Here We Are: Feminism for the Real World*. Chapel Hill, NC: Algonquin Young Readers, 2017.

Sam Killermann. *A Guide to Gender: The Social Justice Advocate's Handbook*. Austin, TX: Impetus Books, 2017.

Michael Kimmel. *Angry White Men: American Masculinity at the End of an Era*. New York, NY: Nation Books, 2013.

Michael Kimmel. *Guyland: The Perilous World Where Boys Become Men*. New York, NY: Harper, 2008.

Kate Manne. *Down Girl: The Logic of Misogyny*. Oxford, United Kingdom: Oxford University Press, 2017.

Jack Myers. *The Future of Men: Men on Trial*. Oakland, CA: Inkshares, 2016.

C. J. Pascoe and Tristan Bridges. *Exploring Masculinities: Identity, Inequality, Continuity and Change*. United Kingdom: Oxford University Press, 2015.

Hanna Rosin. *The End of Men: And the Rise of Women*. New York, NY: Riverhead Books, 2012.

Kristen Schilt. *Just One of the Guys?: Transgender Men and the Persistence of Gender Inequality*. Chicago, IL: University of Chicago Press, 2011.

Shira Tarrant. *Men Speak Out: Views on Gender, Sex, and Power*. United Kingdom: Routledge, 2013.

Rylan Jay Testa, Deborah Coolhart, and Jayme Peta. *The Gender Quest Workbook: A Guide for Teens and Young Adults Exploring Gender Identity*. Oakland, CA: Instant Help, 2015.

Index

F

Families and Work Institute
survey, 132–135
feminism, and inclusiveness,
80–82, 84–92
FIFA, 69
Finding Home, 86
Finucane, Cameron, 44
FTSE 100 companies, 62, 65

G

gay, how it differs from queer, 124
Gelfer, Joseph, 122–126
gender, explanation of, 14, 22
gender awareness, age of, 150, 151
gender fluidity, explanation of, 125
gender indifference/irrelevance,
47–51
gender-neutral pronouns, 15, 153,
158, 159
gender panic, 29
gender parity, international
overview of, 136–139
gender queer people, 24
gender roles, overview of
traditional, 26–31
Generation Y, 43–46
Girl Rising, 89–90
Good Men Project, 47, 97
Google manifesto, 137–138
Grigson, Natalie, 77
*Guns and the Decline of the Young
Man*, 98

H

Half the Sky, 90
Hawkins, John, 26–31
Heritage Foundation, 16
Herzog, Katie, 155–161
Holy Wives, The, 90
Honor Diaries, 91–92
honor killings, 91
Hooligan Sparrow, 88
human sex ratio, 145, 146–149
Hunting Ground, The, 86–87

I

India, traditional gender roles in,
22
India's Daughter, 89
infanticide, 85, 87–88
intersex, 15, 33, 34, 37, 157, 158
It's a Girl, 88

J

Jope, Alan, 56–61

K

Kalymnos, 27
Killermann, Sam, 23
King, Tania, 150–154
Kott, Lidia Jean, 43–46
Krafft-Ebing, Richard von, 111

L

lesbians, nonbinary identity as
threat to, 155–161

Y